Frommer's®

W9-CDL-962

Rome
day BY **day**™
2nd Edition

by Sylvie Hogg

WILEY
Wiley Publishing, Inc.

Contents

Published by:

Wiley Publishing, Inc.

111 River St.
Hoboken, NJ 07030-5774

Copyright © 2009 Wiley Publishing, Inc., Hoboken, New Jersey. All rights reserved. No part of this publication may be reproduced, stored in a retrieval system or transmitted in any form or by any means, electronic, mechanical, photocopying, recording, scanning or otherwise, except as permitted under Sections 107 or 108 of the 1976 United States Copyright Act, without either the prior written permission of the Publisher, or authorization through payment of the appropriate per-copy fee to the Copyright Clearance Center, 222 Rosewood Drive, Danvers, MA 01923, 978/750-8400, fax 978/646-8600. Requests to the Publisher for permission should be addressed to the Legal Department, Wiley Publishing, Inc., 10475 Crosspoint Blvd., Indianapolis, IN 46256, 317/572-3447, fax 317/572-4355, or online at http://www.wiley.com/go/permissions.

Wiley, the Wiley Publishing logo, and Day by Day are trademarks or registered trademarks of John Wiley & Sons, Inc. and/or its affiliates. Frommer's is a trademark or registered trademark of Arthur Frommer. Used under license. All other trademarks are the property of their respective owners. Wiley Publishing, Inc. is not associated with any product or vendor mentioned in this book.

ISBN 978-0-470-38172-4

Editors: Matthew Brown & Cate Latting
Production Editor: Lindsay Conner
Photo Editor: Richard Fox
Cartographer: Roberta Stockwell
Production by Wiley Indianapolis Composition Services

For information on our other products and services or to obtain technical support, please contact our Customer Care Department within the U.S. at 800/762-2974, outside the U.S. at 317/572-3993 or fax 317/572-4002.

Wiley also publishes its books in a variety of electronic formats. Some content that appears in print may not be available in electronic formats.

Manufactured in China

5   4   3   2   1

A Note from the Editorial Director

Organizing your time. That's what this guide is all about.

Other guides give you long lists of things to see and do and then expect you to fit the pieces together. The Day by Day guides are different. These guides tell you the best of everything, and then they show you how to see it *in the smartest, most time-efficient way*. Our authors have designed detailed itineraries organized by time, neighborhood, or special interest. And each tour comes with a bulleted map that takes you from stop to stop.

Hoping to relive the glory days of ancient Rome or to tour the highlights of Vatican City? Planning a walk through Piazza Navona or a whirlwind tour of the very best that Rome has to offer? Whatever your interest or schedule, the Day by Days give you the smartest routes to follow. Not only do we take you to the top attractions, hotels, and restaurants, but we also help you access those special moments that locals get to experience—those "finds" that turn tourists into travelers.

The Day by Days are also your top choice if you're looking for one complete guide for all your travel needs. The best hotels and restaurants for every budget, the greatest shopping values, the wildest nightlife—it's all here.

Why should you trust our judgment? Because our authors personally visit each place they write about. They're an independent lot who say what they think and would never include places they wouldn't recommend to their best friends. They're also open to suggestions from readers. If you'd like to contact them, please send your comments our way at feedback@frommers.com, and we'll pass them on.

Enjoy your Day by Day guide—the most helpful travel companion you can buy. And have the trip of a lifetime.

Warm regards,

Kelly Regan

Kelly Regan, Editorial Director
Frommer's Travel Guides

About the Author

Californian **Sylvie Hogg** spent most of her 20s leading tours through ancient Rome and the Vatican (what else do you do with a Classics degree from Dartmouth?) and has been writing about Rome and Italy for various U.S. and U.K. print and Web publications and audio guides for the past 10 years. She is the lead author of *MTV Italy,* which took bronze in the Lowell Thomas Award's "Best Guidebook" category in 2007, and is currently at work co-authoring the first edition of *Italy Day by Day.* Sylvie hangs her cappello in Kansas City these days, but Rome is where her soul always feels most at home.

Acknowledgments

I dedicate this book wholly to the loving memory of my dear friend, hilarious partner-in-crime, and Roman brother, Fabrizio Cuneo (1966–2008). *Caro Fabri, la mia amatissima Roma ha perso un grande pezzo del suo cuore.*

An Additional Note

Please be advised that travel information is subject to change at any time— and this is especially true of prices. We therefore suggest that you write or call ahead for confirmation when making your travel plans. The authors, editors, and publisher cannot be held responsible for the experiences of readers while traveling. Your safety is important to us, however, so we encourage you to stay alert and be aware of your surroundings.

Star Ratings, Icons & Abbreviations

Every hotel, restaurant, and attraction listing in this guide has been ranked for quality, value, service, amenities, and special features using a **star-rating system.** Hotels, restaurants, attractions, shopping, and nightlife are rated on a scale of zero stars (recommended) to three stars (exceptional). In addition to the star-rating system, we also use a **kids icon** to point out the best bets for families. Within each tour, we recommend cafes, bars, or restaurants where you can take a break. Each of these stops appears in a shaded box marked with a coffee-cup-shaped bullet 🍵.

The following **abbreviations** are used for credit cards:

AE	American Express	DISC	Discover	V	Visa
DC	Diners Club	MC	MasterCard		

Frommers.com

Now that you have this guidebook to help you plan a great trip, visit our website at **www.frommers.com** for additional travel information on more than 4,000 destinations. We update features regularly to give you instant access to the most current trip-planning information available. At Frommers.com, you'll find scoops on the best airfares, lodging rates, and car rental bargains. You can even book your travel online through our reliable travel booking partners. Other popular features include:

- Online updates of our most popular guidebooks
- Vacation sweepstakes and contest giveaways
- Newsletters highlighting the hottest travel trends
- Podcasts, interactive maps, and up-to-the-minute events listings
- Opinionated blog entries by Arthur Frommer himself
- Online travel message boards with featured travel discussions

A Note on Prices

In the "Take a Break" and "Best Bets" sections of this book, we have used a system of dollar signs to show a range of costs for 1 night in a hotel (the price of a double-occupancy room) or the cost of an entree at a restaurant. Use the following table to decipher the dollar signs:

Cost	Hotels	Restaurants
$	under $100	under $10
$$	$100–$200	$10–$20
$$$	$200–$300	$20–$30
$$$$	$300–$400	$30–$40
$$$$$	over $400	over $40

An Invitation to the Reader

In researching this book, we discovered many wonderful places—hotels, restaurants, shops, and more. We're sure you'll find others. Please tell us about them, so we can share the information with your fellow travelers in upcoming editions. If you were disappointed with a recommendation, we'd love to know that, too. Please write to:

Frommer's Rome Day by Day, 2nd Edition
Wiley Publishing, Inc. • 111 River St. • Hoboken, NJ 07030-5774

15 Favorite
Moments

15 Favorite **Moments**

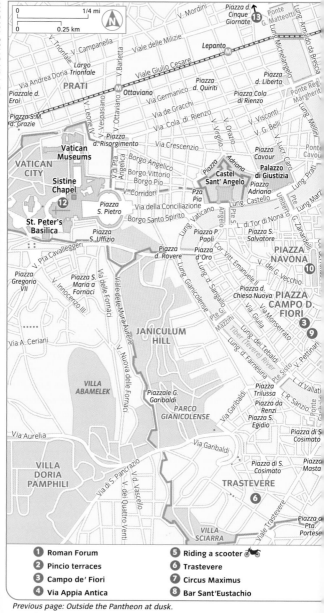

0		1/4 mi		
0	0.25 km			

V. Mordini

Piazza d. Cinque Giornate

Ponte G. Matteotti

Lung. Armando da Brescia

V. Trionfale V. Campanella

Viale delle Milizie

Lepanto M

Lung. Michelangelo

Largo Trionfale

V. Barletta

Viale Giulio Cesare

Ponte Reg. Margherit

Via Andrea Doria

PRATI

Ottaviano M

Piazza d. Quiriti

Piazza Cola di Rienzo

Piazza d. Liberta

Piazzale d. Eroi

Via Germanico

Piazza S. M. d. Grazie

V. Leone IV

V. Vespasiano

V. Ottaviano

Via de Gracchi

Via de. Cola. di. Rienzo

V. Orazio

V. Virgilio

V. Visconti

V. G. Belli

V. Luci. Caro

Ponte Cavou

Vatican Museums

V. di Pta. Angelica

Piazza d. Risorgimento

Borgo Angelico

Via Crescenzio

Adriana

Piazza Cola

Piazza Cavour

VATICAN CITY

Sistine Chapel

St. Peter's Basilica

Borgo Vittorio

Borgo Pio

V. Corridori

Castel Sant' Angelo

Palazzo di Giustizia

Piazza Adriana

Lung. Castello

Umberto

Lung. Prati

Ponte

Lung. Mellini

12

Piazza S. Pietro

Pza Pia

Via della Conciliazione

Borgo Santo Spirito

Lung. Vaticano

Angelo

Ponte S.

L. di Tor di Nona

Lung. d. Zanardelli

Piazza S. Uffizio

Piazza S. Uffizio

Piazza P. Paoli

Piazza d'Oro

Piazza S. Salvatore

V. Pta Cavalleggeri

Piazza S. Maria a Fornaci

Via delle Fornaci

Piazza d. Rovere

Cor. Vitt. Emanuele II

V. dei G. Vecchio

PIAZZA NAVONA

10

Piazza Gregorio VII

V. Innocenzo III

Viale delle Mura Aurelie

Lung. Gianicolense

Pte G.

Piazza d. Chiesa Nuova

PIAZZA CAMPO D. FIORI

3 **9**

Via A. Ceriani

V. Nuova delle Fornaci

JANICULUM HILL

Lung. d. Sangallo

Mazzini

Via Monserrato

Lung. dei Tebaldi

Via Giulia

V. Pettinari

Tiber Tevere River

Pte Sisto

L. R. Sanzio

L. d. Vallati

VILLA ABAMELEK

Piazzale G. Garibaldi

Lung. d. Farnesina

Piazza Trilussa

Piazza da Renzi

Ponte

PARCO GIANICOLENSE

Via Garibaldi

Piazza S. Egidio

Piazza di S Cosimato

Via Aurelia

VILLA DORIA PAMPHILI

Via di S. Pancrazio

V. d. Vascello

Via Garibaldi

Piazza di S. Cosimato

Piazza Masta

V. del Quattro Venti

TRASTEVERE

6

Piazza a Pta. Portese

VILLA SCIARRA

Viale Trastevere

13

1 Roman Forum	**5** Riding a scooter 🛵	
2 Pincio terraces	**6** Trastevere	
3 Campo de' Fiori	**7** Circus Maximus	
4 Via Appia Antica	**8** Bar Sant'Eustachio	

Previous page: Outside the Pantheon at dusk.

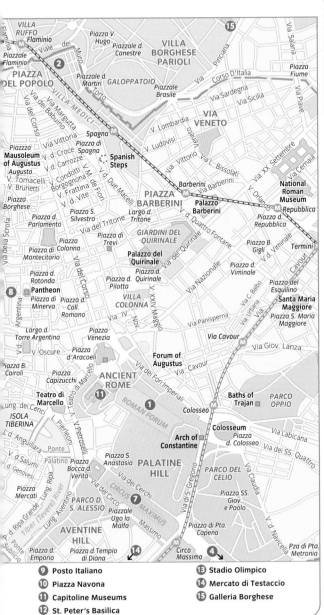

When it comes to experiencing the best of Rome, sun-drenched days at the Colosseum are only the beginning—the Eternal City virtually bombards you with ways to enjoy yourself, from the visual to the gastronomical. With its unrivalled concentration of art and history, romantic scenery, and vibrant people, Rome embraces all with a monumental, irresistible charm. Here are the most sublime moments in our ongoing love affair.

① Gazing over the ruins of the Roman Forum and Palatine from the Capitoline Hill terraces in the evening and, from there, strolling down Via dei Fori Imperiali, where strategically placed floodlights cast dramatic glows over solitary columns and the arches of the Colosseum. The ruins of Rome at night are truly, disarmingly spectacular. *See p 24*.

② Taking your lover to the Pincio terraces, whose theatrical ivy-covered stone balustrades and view are virtually unchanged since the Renaissance, when maidens, courtiers, and the occasional knave no doubt met here for trysts and double-crossings. *See p 45*.

③ After a long day of sightseeing, joining the rest of Rome for an aperitivo at one of the outdoor bars on Campo de' Fiori. Take a seat, praise Bacchus for having created inexpensive, drinkable wine, and watch the world go by. *See p 56*.

④ Treading the ancient paving stones along the leafy Via Appia Antica, and leaving the hustle and bustle of the *centro* far behind. From the catacombs to the ruined villas of Roman patricians, there's a quiet but heavy sense of history here. Umbrella pines and farmland perfume the air, transporting you back to the time when this was Rome's *Regina Viarum* (Queen of Roads). *See p 97*.

⑤ Riding a scooter, half-fearing for your life, over the broad cobblestone avenues of Rome's archaeological areas, past umbrella pines and

The Pincio terraces make for a romantic rendezvous.

Romans enjoying an alfresco lunch at a sunny trattoria.

2,000-year-old ruins. A thrill ride and history lesson all in one.

6 Wandering the untouristed, narrow back streets of Trastevere and discovering shops, eateries, and slices of local life not listed in any guidebook. Separated from the rest of the old city by the river, this picturesque neighborhood has been able to maintain its own identity since ancient times, when it was simply called Trans Tiberim ("across the Tiber"). *See p 58.*

7 Standing along the high western rim of the Circus Maximus and absorbing the view from among the umbrella pines across to the ruins of Palatine Hill. As you do, imagine being one of the 300,000 fans cheering on the raucous, ancient Roman chariot races. *See p 27.*

8 Mastering the art of taking a caffè at a real Roman bar. Walk into the bar, greeting all with a smile and *"Buon giorno."* Pay for your drink at the *cassa*, and take your receipt to the bar counter. Slip a 10- or 20-cent tip on top of the receipt, and place your order with the *barista*. Drink your coffee as the Romans do—standing up at the bar.

9 Buying Italian leather shoes that look and feel as good as big-name designer—for a fraction of the price. Italy's sophisticated,

lesser-known labels are a much more authentic souvenir than Gucci or Prada, and they'll still make your friends back home green with envy. Posto Italiano is a good place to start. *See p 87.*

10 Spending hours over lunch or dinner at a typical Roman trattoria or pizzeria, with a steady, wonderfully affordable flow of wine, water, and delicious food. Look for such Roman classics as *spaghetti alla carbonara* (pasta with bacon, black pepper, and eggs) or *saltimbocca alla romana* (thin slices of veal with cheese, ham, and sage). *See p 101.*

11 Going to the Capitoline Museum's Palazzo Nuovo in late afternoon on a crisp winter day, when no one else is there. Your only companions are half-drunk, smirking fauns and busts of Hadrian and Homer. *See p 31.*

12 Taking your first step over the threshold of St. Peter's Basilica. When the ethereal light of the low afternoon sun is broken into celestial beams by the basilica's well-placed windows, Bernini's stained-glass dove of the Holy Spirit against the church's terminal apse flickers with searing tones of amber. *See p 48.*

13 Going to a Roma or Lazio soccer *(calcio)* game on a sunny Sunday afternoon and joining in the

Soccer fans wave colorful team scarves at a match in Stadio Olimpico.

infectious, unbridled exhilaration that floods the stadium when the home team scores. You're likely to be hugged and spun around by complete strangers. *See p 132.*

⑭ Mixing with locals at the lively Mercato di Testaccio. No other market in the city has such a strong sense of community: Yuppies and jovial retirees shuffle from stall to stall, passionately debating the latest political scandal—or *calcio* (football) league standings—while they expertly pick out the freshest culinary delights.

Perhaps more so than any other Roman neighborhood, Testaccio has a salt-of-the-earth flavor drawn from its working-class slaughterhouse past. *See p 74.*

⑮ Encountering Bernini's sculptures at Galleria Borghese. Grimace in determination as *David* does against daunting adversary Goliath, or gape at the amazing detail of *Apollo* and *Daphne*. The paintings and ceiling frescoes throughout the gallery make for colorful counterpoints. *See p 30.* ●

Bernini statue amid the ceiling frescoes at Villa Borghese.

The Best **in One Day**

| 0 | | 1/4 mi |
| 0 | 0.25 km | |

1. Campidoglio (Capitoline Hill)
2. Roman Forum
3. Colosseum
4. Imperial Fora
5. Vittoriano
6' Caffè Italia
7. Pantheon
8. Vatican Museums

Previous page: Columns at the Pantheon.

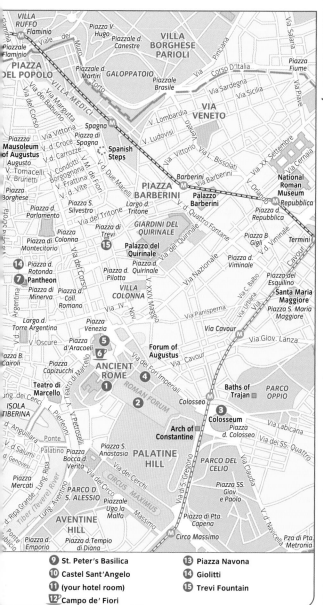

9 St. Peter's Basilica
10 Castel Sant'Angelo
11 (your hotel room)
12 Campo de' Fiori
13 Piazza Navona
14 Giolitti
15 Trevi Fountain

Seeing the top sights of Rome in 1 day requires an early start, discipline, and a bit of stamina, but it's actually quite doable. This "greatest hits" itinerary begins with an overview of the highlights of ancient Rome; after lunch, cross town and spend a few hours at the Vatican. Conclude your day with a leisurely evening walking tour of the gorgeously floodlit fountains and piazzas of the *centro storico*. START: Take bus 30, 40, 62, 64, 70, 87, 95, 170, 492, or 628 to Piazza dell'Ara Coeli and climb the stairs to Piazza del Campidoglio.

Travel Tip

Seasonal opening hours of some attractions may require modification of the itinerary below: For example, because of the Vatican Museums' shorter winter hours, from November to February, you'll need to do the Vatican in the morning and ancient Rome in the afternoon.

❶ ★★★ Campidoglio (Capitoline Hill). The most sacred of Rome's hills was given its present look in the 1500s, when Michelangelo designed the star-patterned square and surrounding buildings of the Capitoline Museums (see p 31, bullet ❻). The bronze statue of Marcus Aurelius in the center of the piazza is a copy; the 2nd-century-A.D. original is inside the museum. The western slopes of the hill, with their steep red *tufa* walls and tangled vegetation, still look much the same as they would have in the primordial days before the rise of Rome. Don't miss the majestic view of the Roman Forum from the south-facing terraces on either side of the bell-towered Palazzo Senatorio (city hall). 🕐 *15–30 min. Also gorgeous—and deserted—at night. Bus: 30, 40, 62, 64, 70, 87, 170, 492, or 571.*

❷ ★★★ Roman Forum. While the Forum is not one of the better-preserved archaeological sites of ancient Rome, it is the most historically significant. The Forum was the nerve center of the most powerful Western civilization in history for the better part of a thousand years, where political decisions were made, public speeches were heard, and market activities took place. The remains here—of 2,000-year-old

The ruins of the Roman forum were excavated in the 19th century.

The Colosseum takes on a spectral glow at dusk.

temples, law courts, and victory monuments—are impressive but skeletal, and can be difficult to decipher. ⏲ *30–45 min. See p 24, bullet* **7** *for full details.*

3 ★★★ **Colosseum.** The Flavian amphitheater (A.D. 72–80) never fails to impress—for its elegant, enduring bulk, and its disturbing former function as a theater of slaughter. At the height of the Roman Empire, games were held almost every other day; in times of special celebration, games could last for weeks or months on end. Free *tesserae* (tickets) were distributed to about 65,000 Romans, who could be seated in the arena in a matter of minutes, thanks to an efficient system of 80 numbered *vomitoria* (entrance/exit passageways). Against slashing swords and gnashing lions' teeth, gladiators and *bestiarii* (animal fighters) fought to the death, hoping to someday win their freedom. (In the Colosseum's 400-year history, fewer than 100 men ever did.) A visit inside the massive structure is certainly rewarding, but if you're pressed for time or cash, a walk around the exterior is fine. If there's a long queue, buy your tickets at the Palatine (p 26, bullet **8**) and go straight to the turnstiles. ⏲ *30–45 min. See p 26, bullet* **10** *for full details.*

4 ★★ **Imperial Fora.** Mussolini blazed the broad thoroughfare of Via dell'Impero—now Via dei Fori Imperiali—to trumpet the glories of his ancient forebears and propagate his own ambitions of empire. Along the east side of the boulevard, the ruins of the forums built by emperors Nerva, Augustus, and Trajan can be seen protruding from the ancient street level, 7.6m (25 ft.) below. On the west side, near the Colosseum, don't miss the fascinating marble maps (also from the Fascist period) charting the spread of the Roman Empire, which reached as far east as Iran (Parthia). ⏲ *30 min. Via dei Fori Imperiali.*

5 ★ **Vittoriano.** Locals revile the 100-year-old monument to Victor Emanuel II, the first king of united Italy, as a tasteless and over-the-top neoclassical "typewriter," but tourists can't seem to take their eyes off the plus-size marble confection on the south side of Piazza Venezia. Take the elevator to the uppermost level, the Terrazza delle Quadrighe, for the most thrilling view in Rome. ⏲ *30–45 min. Admission for upper terrace only 7€. Daily 10am–4:30pm. Bus: 30, 40, 60, 62, 64, 70, 85, 87, or 492.*

6 ★ **Caffè Italia.** Take a breather at this alfresco cafe halfway up the summit of the Vittoriano, to the left of the gigantic bronze statue of the king on horseback. *Il Vittoriano.* ☎ 06-6780905. $–$$.

7 ★★★ **Pantheon.** As the best-preserved and most elegant ancient building in the city—if not the world—the Pantheon ("temple to all gods") merits multiple visits. It was designed and possibly built by Hadrian from A.D. 118 to 125, in a form governed by circles and squares—shapes which, as Vitruvius wrote (and Leonardo later immortalized in his drawing the *Vitruvian Man*), the human body most naturally occupies. The Pantheon's perfectly hemispherical, poured-concrete dome is 43m (141 ft.) tall and wide—1m (3 ft.) wider than the dome of St. Peter's. ⏱ *15–30 min. See p 54, bullet* **11**. *Take a taxi from the Pantheon to the Vatican Museums.*

8 ★★★ **Vatican Museums.** After lunch, the crowds have left the Vatican, making it much more

Michelangelo's Pietà.

pleasant to explore. Stay focused, however, and make sure you see the starring ancient sculptures—the gut-wrenching emotion and dynamism of *Laocoon,* the transcendent composure of *Apollo Belvedere*—in the Pio-Clementine section of the museums, and then hightail it for the Vatican's biggest guns, Raphael's *stanze* and Michelangelo's frescoes in the Sistine Chapel. The art here, by two of the greatest painters in history, is a triumph of Renaissance achievement, bold in color, lofty in concept, and monumental in scale. ⏱ *1½ hr. See p 49, bullet* **6** *for a more comprehensive review.*

9 ★★★ **St. Peter's Basilica.** The incomprehensibly voluminous Vatican basilica is packed with incalculable riches, from the marble and gold that cover its every surface to masterpieces like Michelangelo's *Pietà* and Bernini's *Baldacchino.* ⏱ *30 min. Dome visit not absolutely necessary. See p 48, bullet* **2**.

10 ★★ **Castel Sant'Angelo.** You probably won't have the time or energy to go inside, but the view of this mausoleum-turned-fortress, from Ponte Sant'Angelo—where angels by Bernini wince and moan—is not to be missed. ⏱ *15 min. See p 53, bullet* **1** *for full details.*

11 **Your hotel room.** By now, it's 4 or 5pm—a good time to return to your hotel, rest your feet, and freshen up before heading back out for dinner and your evening walking tour. Just don't crash completely. If it's after 5pm, and you're feeling energetic, skip the hotel and proceed directly to **12**, below.

12 ★★★ **Campo de' Fiori.** By early evening (6–6:30pm), this square in the very heart of the

ancient athletic stadium of Domitian, boasts Bernini's fantastic Fountain of the Four Rivers and Borromini's church of Sant'Agnese in Agone, as well as the smaller Fontana del Moro and Fontana di Nettuno. There are also a number of cafes to tempt you with after-dinner treats—it's unabashedly touristy, but the setting sure is pretty. ⏱ *20–30 min. See p 38, bullet* ❶*, and p 53, bullet* ❻*. Bus: 30, 40, 62, 64, 70, 87, 116, or 492.*

⑭ ★★ **Giolitti.** At the city's best-loved gelato shop, the setting is elegant and the ritual is fun. Pay the cashier up front, then negotiate your way through the crowds in back, where gracious servers scoop up enormous helpings of almost 100 flavors. *Via degli Uffici del Vicario 40.* ☎ *06-6991243. $.*

⑮ ★★★ **Trevi Fountain.** Rome's most celebrated fountain, designed by Nicola Salvi and built from 1732–62, is impressive enough during the day, but at night, the floodlights make it look cleaner and doubly spectacular—so gorgeous that you won't even mind the crowds. ⏱ *20 min. Piazza di Trevi. Bus: 62, 85, 95, 175, or 492.*

The Trevi Fountain lit up at night.

centro storico is abuzz with all kinds of people taking an *aperitivo* at the many outdoor bars. (I recommend **Vineria Reggio** and **Taverna del Campo,** p 114.) Later in the evening, it's a younger scene. Campo de' Fiori and nearby Piazza Navona, the starting points of your evening tour, are also prime zones for dinner. ⏱ *1 hr. See p 101. Bus: 30, 40, 62, 64, 70, 87, 116, or 492. $–$$.*

⑬ ★★★ **Piazza Navona.** The most famous baroque square in Rome, built on the site of the

St. Peter's Basilica fronting St. Peter's Square.

The Best **in Two Days**

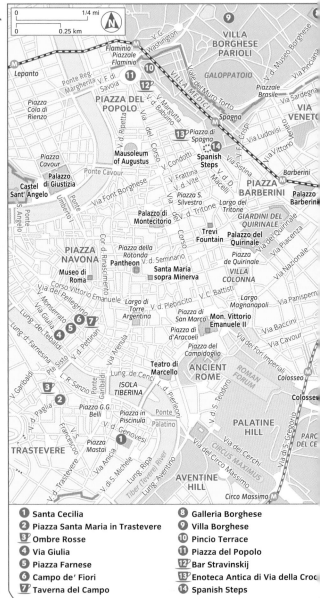

1 Santa Cecilia
2 Piazza Santa Maria in Trastevere
3 Ombre Rosse
4 Via Giulia
5 Piazza Farnese
6 Campo de' Fiori
7 Taverna del Campo
8 Galleria Borghese
9 Villa Borghese
10 Pincio Terrace
11 Piazza del Popolo
12 Bar Stravinskij
13 Enoteca Antica di Via della Croce
14 Spanish Steps

On your second day, spend the morning wandering the picturesque squares and alleys of Trastevere and Campo de' Fiori, Rome's oldest and most authentic quarters. Have lunch, and then cross town to feast your eyes on the crown jewels of baroque art in the Galleria Borghese. Go for a stroll through the Villa Borghese, making your way to the Pincio terraces and their enchanting view over the city and the Vatican. Finish the day by visiting the elegant Tridente district below, where such *dolce vita* activities as shopping, drinking, and eating abound. Allow 2½ hours for the morning tour of Trastevere and Campo de' Fiori. START: **Take bus 23, 271, or 280 to Lungotevere degli Anguillara, and then walk to Piazza di Santa Cecilia; or take bus H, 780, or tram 8 to Piazza G. G. Belli, and walk.**

① ★ **Santa Cecilia.** This incredibly peaceful basilica—an 18th-century reworking of a medieval church—is dedicated to the patron saint of music, who was martyred here in the 3rd century A.D. Inside, altar mosaics dazzle, and fragments of Pietro Cavallini's wonderful 13th-century fresco of the *Last Judgment* can be seen at limited times. Cecilia was exhumed from her tomb in the crypt here in 1599, long enough for Stefano Maderno to sculpt the lovely (but disturbing—her throat is slashed) statue of the saint's still-uncorrupted body below the altar. The church is one of the most popular in Rome for weddings, evidenced by omnipresent grains of rice on the ground near the front door. ⏲ *20 min. Piazza di Santa Cecilia.* ☎ *06-5899289. Daily 9:30am–12:30pm, 4–6:30pm. Cavallini frescoes: Tues,*

Thurs 10am–noon, Sun 11:30am–12:30pm. Bus: 23, 271, 280, or H. Tram: 3 or 8.

② ★★ **Piazza and Basilica di Santa Maria in Trastevere.** The first church in Rome dedicated to the Virgin Mary is spectacular inside and out, with a landmark Romanesque brick bell tower, colorful frescoes, mosaics, and loads of recycled ancient marbles. The eponymous square in front of the church acts as a kind of common living room for the neighborhood—it seems that every resident of Trastevere crosses the wide expanse of cobblestones here at some point during the day. See also p 39, bullet **⑧**, and p 43, bullet **⑧**. ⏲ *20 min. Piazza Santa Maria in Trastevere.* ☎ *06-5814802. Daily 7:30am–9pm. Bus: 23, 271, 280, or H. Tram: 8.*

A cafe in Trastevere.

3 ★ **Ombre Rosse.** This cafe with a porchlike view over a charming piazza is more stylish than the average neighborhood bar, but still frequented by born-and-bred, local *trasteverini*, and perfect for cappuccino-sipping and people-watching. *Piazza Sant' Egidio 12.* ☎ *06-5884155. $–$$.*

4 ★★ **Via Giulia.** Bearing straight toward the Vatican from Ponte Sisto, this former pilgrim route is home to many art galleries and high-end, original boutiques. Via Giulia's most fetching feature is an arch—with overgrown ivy draped luxuriously toward the pitch-black cobblestones—that spans the road behind Palazzo Farnese. ⊕ *15 min. Bus: 23, 271, or 280.*

5 ★★ **Piazza Farnese.** Sophisticated and regal Piazza Farnese is where locals come to read the newspaper or to push a stroller in peace, against the stately, yellow-brick backdrop of 16th-century Palazzo Farnese. The sleepy square seems a world away—in reality, it's only a block—from the hubbub of Campo de' Fiori. See also p 39, bullet **10**, and p 57, bullet **3**. ⊕ *15 min. Bus: 23, 30, 40, 62, 64, 70, 87, 116, 271, 492, or 571. Tram: 8.*

6 ★★★ **Campo de' Fiori.** Rome's market square par excellence, the Campo is the perfect embodiment of the myth of Italy. Every morning from Monday to Saturday, the square hosts a lively fruit, vegetable, and trinket bazaar. By early evening, where grocery shoppers eyed *pachino* tomatoes a few hours before, Rome's bright young things are scoping out each other over sparkling wine and effervescent conversation, indulging in the carefree atmosphere of this always busy outdoor salon. See also p 39, bullet **11**, and p 56, bullet **1**. ⊕ *20–30 min. Bus: 23, 30, 40, 62, 64, 70, 87, 116, or 492. Tram: 8.*

7 **Taverna del Campo.** Break for lunch on or around Campo de' Fiori before beginning the second part of the day's tour. For savory pizza-bread sandwiches and piazza views, Taverna del Campo can't be beat (p 114). *$$.*

8 ★★★ **Galleria Borghese.** Reel in amazement at sculptures by Bernini (and other masterpieces) at one of the world's most outstanding small museums. Visits must be booked at least 1 day in advance: Go for the 1 or 3pm time slot. See also p 30, bullet **3**. ⊕ *1 hr.*

Tomatoes and zucchini for sale at the market in Campo de' Fiori.

The Spanish Steps are one of the city's favorite gathering places.

Piazzale Museo Borghese. ☎ 06-32810. Admission 8.50€ plus 2€ booking fee. Tues–Sun 9am–7pm (last visit 5pm). Bus: 116 or 910.

⑨ ★★ Villa Borghese. Go for a relaxing stroll among the refreshing greenery of Rome's most central public park. Boats can be rented at the picturesque *laghetto*. See also p 92. ⏱ *30 min. Daily 6am–sunset. Metro: Spagna. Bus: 52, 53, 63, 116, or 910. Tram: 3 or 19.*

⑩ ★★★ Pincio Terrace. Hearts flutter at the impressive perspective on the Vatican from this panoramic spot above Piazza del Popolo. It's gloriously sun-filled by day, ultraromantic by night. See also p 45, bullet ③. ⏱ *15 min. Metro: Flaminio.*

⑪ ★★ Piazza del Popolo. Romans and tourists alike bask in the late-afternoon sun that floods this vast, traffic-free oval space just below the Pincio. Graced in the center by a massive, hieroglyphed pink granite obelisk, the "Square of the People" is wonderfully elegant and uncluttered—perfect for idling and gelato-licking, and a fitting introduction to the good-life in Tridente district, which spreads out pronglike to the south. See also p 38, bullet ④, and p 61, bullet ①. ⏱ *15 min. Metro: Flaminio.*

⑫ ★★ Bar Stravinskij. Forget the cheesy sidewalk cafes of Via Veneto—these days, celebs hounded by the paparazzi duck into this (pricey) bar inside the glamorous Hotel de Russie. In warm weather, sit outside in the gorgeous interior garden, sloping up toward the Pincio; in winter, get cozy at the piano bar's indoor tables. *Via del Babuino 9.* ☎ *06-328881. $$$–$$$$.*

⑬ ★★ Enoteca Antica di Via della Croce. For a more budget-friendly snack, grab a barstool or sidewalk seat and enjoy some wine and tantalizing plates of meats, cheeses, and olives at this friendly spot. A favorite of expats living in Rome. *Via della Croce 76B.* ☎ *06-6790896. $$.*

⑭ ★★★ Spanish Steps. Fortunately, the sweeping beauty of the Scalinata di Piazza di Spagna transcends the sometimes-ugly crowds of tourists that populate the square day and night. The climb to the high terrace covers 12 curving flights of steps of varying width—you'll trip if you don't watch where your feet are—but the view from the top is exhilarating. Come between 2 and 6am, and you'll enjoy that rarest of Roman treats—having the fabulous stage of the Spanish Steps to yourself. See also p 63, bullet ⑪. ⏱ *30 min. Metro: Spagna.*

The Best **in Three Days**

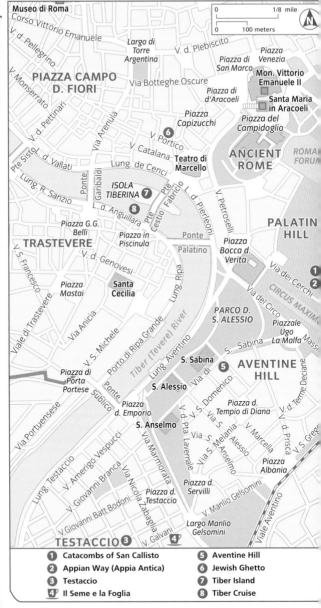

1 Catacombs of San Callisto	**5** Aventine Hill
2 Appian Way (Appia Antica)	**6** Jewish Ghetto
3 Testaccio	**7** Tiber Island
4 Il Seme e la Foglia	**8** Tiber Cruise

One of the best and most surprising things about Rome is how quickly you can escape the urban chaos and enjoy the rustic tranquillity of the city's greener areas, just a few miles away from the tourist hordes. On your third day, visit the catacombs and breathe the spicy, rural air along the history-saturated Appian Way. Then, go for a stroll in the contrasting, adjacent neighborhoods of Testaccio and the Aventine. Finish the day back in the *centro storico* with a walk through the Jewish Ghetto and Tiber Island. (Alternatively, get out of town entirely, and go for a day trip to Ostia Antica or Tivoli. See p 150 and 148.) START: **Take bus 118 or a taxi to the Catacombe di San Callisto on the Appian Way (the entrance is 3.2km/2 miles south of Porta San Sebastiano gate).**

1 ★★★ **Catacombs of San Callisto.** Nineteen kilometers (12 miles) and four levels of hand-dug tunnels make up the underground network of Rome's largest catacombs, home to the tombs of half a million Christians, buried here from the 1st to the 4th centuries A.D. Deep within the complex, a labyrinth of 9m-high (30-ft.) tunnels, whose walls are perforated up to the ceiling with *loculi* (tomb niches), is especially impressive (and uncannily reminiscent of college library stacks). See also p 46. ⏱ *45 min. Via Appia Antica 110.* ☎ *06-5130151. Admission 6€. Open Thurs–Tues 8:30am–noon, 2:30–5pm. Bus: 118.*

A corridor in the Catacombs of San Callisto.

2 ★★★ **Appian Way.** Few places in Rome transport you to ancient times as well as the Via Appia Antica, whose black basalt cobblestones, still bearing the wheel ruts of ancient cart traffic, stretch south of the city from Porta San Sebastiano. A few miles from the city walls, a rustic, agrarian landscape opens up on either side of the 4th-century-B.C. highway; the scenery is scattered with imposing or modest remains of ancient tombs and villas, and shepherds drive flocks of sheep from pasture to pasture, right across the "Queen of Roads." Even the scent of the Appian Way is ripe with antiquity: Once you smell it, the combination of bright notes of umbrella pine needles, musty sunbaked brick and marble, and the acrid pungency of leaves burning in farmyards becomes indelible in your memory. See also p 94. ⏱ *1 hr. Bus: 118.*

3 ★★ **Testaccio.** Anchored by an artificial hill made of ancient pottery cast-offs and populated by salt-of-the-earth *romani de' Roma* (and the odd sheep or goat), the authentic neighborhood of Testaccio oozes character. See also p 72. ⏱ *1 hr. Metro: Piramide. Bus: 30, 60, 75, 95, 118, or 170. Tram: 3.*

A wall-fountain at Santa Sabina.

4 ★ **Il Seme e la Foglia.** With views of the old slaughterhouse and the potsherds of Monte Testaccio, this hip corner joint is a great place for a casual, quick lunch of enormous and tasty salads and sandwiches. *Via Galvani 18.* ☎ *06-5743008. $–$$.*

5 ★★★ **Aventine.** Oblivious to the noise of the *centro* below, Aventine Hill is mostly residential, and home to several churches, whose dignified and simple red-brick exteriors and grassy grounds are a welcome contrast from the fussy facades and cramped quarters of many Roman churches. The 5th-century-A.D. church of Santa Sabina is cavernous and calming—a sublime example of the basilican form. ⏱ *1 hr. Metro: Circo Massimo. Bus: 30, 60, 75, 81, 95, 118, 175, or 628. Tram: 3.*

6 ★★ **Jewish Ghetto.** As the area where Roman Jews were confined from the 16th to the 19th centuries, the medieval quarter between the Capitoline and the Tiber has seen its share of dark days. Today, however, the Ghetto is an upbeat, characteristic part of the *centro storico* that many tourists miss. From towering ancient ruins like the Theater of Marcellus, to sculptural gems like the Fountain of the Tortoises in Piazza Mattei, to the triumphant synagogue, this small area has a lot to see. See also p 66. ⏱ *45 min. Bus: 30, 40, 62, 64, 70, 81, 87, 170, 271, 492, or 628. Tram: 8.*

7 ★★ **Tiber Island.** This boat-shaped protuberance in the middle of the river, between the Ghetto and Trastevere, is an oasis of calm; ever since the Greek god of medicine, Aesculapius, washed up here disguised as a snake, the island has been the city's sanctuary of medicine. Check out the lower promenade (water level permitting), with its great views of the ancient bridges nearby. See also p 66. ⏱ *30 min. Bus: 23, 30, 40, 62, 64, 70, 81, 87, 170, 271, 280, 492, or 628. Tram: 8.*

8 ★★ **Tiber Cruise.** If you have time, going for a ride on the Battelli di Roma riverboat service (also known as "Bateaux Rome") is a great way to relax while seeing Rome from the interesting perspective of this historic waterway, now largely overlooked by the modern city. You can cruise all the way up to the Foro Italico (p 131) for a sunset stroll among the Fascist-inspired athletic cult mosaics and statues. ⏱ *1½ hr.* ☎ *06-97745496. www.rexervation.com/crociere.asp. From 12€. Bus: 23, 271, 280, or H. Tram: 8.* ●

Tiber Island is an oasis of calm.

ient Rome

0 — 1/8 mile
0 — 100 meters

- 1 Teatro di Marcello
- 2 Via di Monte Caprino
- 3 Capitoline Hill
- 4 Via dei Fori Imperiali
- 5 Trajan's Markets and Museum of the Imperial Forums
- 6 Bottega del Caffè
- 7 Roman Forum
- 8 Palatine Hill
- 9 Arch of Constantine
- 10 Colosseum
- 11 Domus Aurea
- 12 Circo Massimo
- 13 Terme di Caracalla

Previous page: Bernini's Four Rivers Fountain in Piazza Navona.

In towering brick or crumbling marble, the awe-inspiring ruins of ancient Rome are concentrated in the archaeological park south of the *centro storico*. Here, in an undulating topography drenched in history and dotted with umbrella pines, lie such famed sights as the Forum and the Colosseum, as well as the most sacred hills of Rome, the Capitoline and the Palatine. Bring a bottle of water and a picnic, and wear comfortable shoes for this half- or full-day tour. In summer, avoid these sites during the intense heat of midday.

START: **Take bus 30, 95, 170, or 628 to Via del Teatro Marcello, or take bus 40, 62, 64, 70, 87, or 492 to Via d'Aracoeli or Piazza Venezia, and walk.**

1 ★ Teatro di Marcello. The familiar arches of this 1st-century-B.C. theater, used for plays and concerts, inspired the design of the Colosseum, built 100 years later. *Via del Teatro Marcello.*

2 ★ Via di Monte Caprino. Past shade trees and weathered fountains, this charming path winds its way up the Capitoline Hill's western slope. In 390 B.C., the Gauls attempted to storm the Capitol under cover of darkness and the dense vegetation here, but the sacred geese of Rome, kept in a pen nearby, detected their movement and sounded the alarm, thwarting

The ruins of the Theater of Marcellus.

the raiders. (The Capitoline guard-dogs, who slept through it, were later crucified.)

3 ★★ Capitoline Hill. Analogous to the Acropolis in Athens, this was the citadel and religious nerve center of ancient Rome. Atop this spur of red tufa, augurs monitored the flight of birds for omens, and traitors were hurled from the infamous Tarpeian Rock. The temple of Jupiter here, now lost, dominated the Roman skyline for centuries. Though it was redubbed Campidoglio in the Middle Ages and architecturally restyled during the Renaissance, the Capitoline's air of antiquity remains palpable. Be sure to visit the hill's southern terraces for staggeringly gorgeous views over the Roman Forum. See p 45, bullet **7** for Piazza del Campidoglio, and p 31, bullet **5** for the Capitoline Museum.

4 ★★ Via dei Fori Imperiali. Mussolini created this tree-lined boulevard, running dead-straight from his balcony at Palazzo Venezia to the Colosseum, to showcase the reminders of Rome's glory days and military might. On the east side of the street, from north to south, are the Forums of Trajan, Augustus, and Nerva; on the west side are the Forum of Julius Caesar and the original Roman Forum.

Columns in the Roman Forum, with the Arch of Titus in the background.

⑤ ★★ Trajan's Markets & Museum of the Imperial Forums. Majestic and overtly phallic, the 40m-high (130-ft.) marble Column of Trajan was dedicated in A.D. 113 to commemorate the Romans' victory over Dacia (modern Romania). The ascending spiral band of sculptured reliefs depicts all stages of the military campaign, down to the finest detail. The most dominant feature in Trajan's Forum is the massive, concave-fronted, brick structure known as Trajan's Markets. Built on three levels, the markets were the world's first mall, housing 150 shops and commercial offices. In 2007, part of Trajan's Markets became exhibition space for the new Museum of the Imperial Forums, which has excellent visual displays that help you imagine what these grand public squares and temples used to look like. ⏱ *45 min. Via IV Novembre 94.* ☎ *06-6790048. 6.50€. Daily 9am–6pm. Bus: 30, 40, 62, 64, 70, 85, 87, 95, 170, 175, or 492.*

⑥ Bottega del Caffè. Grab a bite and people-watch at this busy alfresco cafe just up the hill from the Forum (and a world away from the predatory tourist snack carts down there). Pastries, salads, and panini are available, as are wine, beer, coffee, and soft drinks. *Piazza Madonna dei Monti 5 (at Via dei Serpenti).* ☎ *393-9311013. $–$$.*

⑦ ★★★ Roman Forum. The Forum was the beating heart of republican and imperial Rome and the most important civic space in all of Western civilization for much of antiquity. It was here, in temples, basilicas, and markets that range in date from the 6th century B.C. to the 5th century A.D., that the Roman people carried out their daily religious, political, and commercial activities. Today, the Forum is a picturesque and evocative ruin that bears the deep scars of Roman "recycling"—when power over Rome passed from the emperors to the popes, church fathers dismantled the pagan buildings for their precious marble and bronze. From the late Middle Ages, dirt, debris, and cow manure accumulated in the Forum, reaching a height of 9m (30 ft.) by the 1890s, when excavations began.

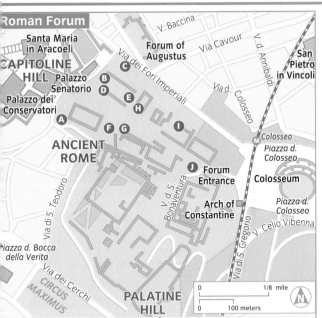

Roman Forum

Santa Maria in Aracoeli

CAPITOLINE HILL

Palazzo Senatorio

Palazzo dei Conservatori

ANCIENT ROME

Via di S. Teodoro

Piazza d. Bocca della Verita

Via dei Cerchi

CIRCUS MAXIMUS

PALATINE HILL

V. Baccina

Via Cavour

Forum of Augustus

Via dei Fori Imperiali

Via d. Annibaldi

V. d. Colosseo

San Pietro in Vincoli

Via d. Colosseo

Colosseo
Piazza d. Colosseo

Colosseum

Piazza d. Colosseo

V. Celio Vibenna

Forum Entrance

Via di S. Bonaventura

Arch of Constantine

Via di S. Gregorio

0 ——— 1/8 mile
0 ——— 100 meters

N

The eight columns of the **7A** ★ **Temple of Saturn** tower over the north end of the Forum, indicating the former height of all the structures here. Nearby, the **7B** ★★ **Arch of Septimius Severus** was erected in the 3rd century A.D. to celebrate that emperor's triumph in Parthia (modern Iran). The tall brick **7C** ★★ **Curia Julia** (29 B.C.) is where the Roman senate met. The low, brown **7D** ★ **Rostra,** or orator's stage, is where Mark Antony addressed friends, Romans, and countrymen. All that's left of the **7E** ★ **Temple of Julius Caesar** (29 B.C.), which once had a hexastyle (six-columned) front, is its podium. Under its green metal roof is the rocky mound where Caesar's funeral pyre burned for 7 days in 44 B.C., culminating in the appearance of a comet. Near here, the picturesque *tria columna* of the **7F** ★★ **Temple of Castor and Pollux** have

helped centuries of poets imagine the splendor of Rome in its heyday. A curved grouping of smaller columns in this area are the ruins of the **7G** ★ **Temple of Vesta,** where the six Vestal Virgins tended the eternal flame of Rome. Opposite, the hexastyle **7H** ★★ **Temple of Antoninus and Faustina** (A.D. 141) survives because it was reconsecrated as a church in the medieval period. The three soaring vaults of the spectacular, 4th-century-A.D. **7I** ★★★ **Basilica of Maxentius** represent only one-third of the law court's original size. Sculptural reliefs on the **7J** ★★ **Arch of Titus** (A.D. 81) glorify the sack of Jerusalem. ⏰ *1 hr. Apr–Oct, go after 2pm to avoid crowds. Largo Romolo e Remo.* ☎ *06-6990110. 11€ (includes Colosseum and Palatine). Daily 9am–1 hr. before sunset. Metro: Colosseo. Bus: 60, 75, 85, 87, 95, or 175.*

The Palatine Hill archaeological park contains the ruins of imperial palaces.

8 ★★ **Palatine Hill.** Back in 753 B.C., Romulus killed Remus and founded Roma on the Palatine. Later, emperors and other ancient bigwigs built their palaces and private entertainment facilities here. Nowadays, it's a sprawling, crowd-free archaeological garden, with plenty of shady spots good for picnicking and cooling off in summer. Be sure to check out the House of Augustus, which was opened to the public in 2008. The Palatine's extensive ruins are time-consuming to explore and not

A relief sculpture on the Arch of Titus depicts the triumphant return of the emperor and the spoils of the great temple of Jerusalem.

very well marked, which is fascinating for some but frustrating for those in a hurry. ⏱ *45 min. Entrances near Arch of Titus and at Via di San Gregorio 30.* ☎ *06-6990110. 11€ (includes Roman Forum and Colosseum). Daily 9am–1 hr. before sunset. Metro: Colosseo. Bus: 60, 75, 85, 87, 95, or 175. Tram: 3.*

9 ★ **Arch of Constantine.** Decorated largely with sculpture looted from earlier emperors' monuments, this arch was dedicated in A.D. 315 to commemorate the Battle of the Milvian Bridge (A.D. 312), in which Constantine defeated his co-emperor, Maxentius, after having a vision of the Christian cross. The superstitious Constantine legalized Christianity in A.D. 313 with the Edict of Milan, ending centuries of persecution.

10 ★★★ **Colosseum.** Occupying the masses' free time with escapist, high-testosterone spectacles, the games at the Flavian amphitheater were the NASCAR of antiquity. Inaugurated in A.D. 80 over the site of Nero's lake, the Colosseum hosted 65,000 fans every other day with its gory contests between men and animals. The enormous scale and masterful architecture of the amphitheater, supported entirely on radial and lateral arches, can be appreciated well enough from the outside, but inside, a modern catwalk allows visitors to stand at the same level where gladiators and hippos once fought to the death. Below, an ingenious system of 32 elevator shafts and trapdoors kept the action constant, replenishing the arena with new combatants and props when one fight ended. In A.D. 523, well after the rise of Christianity, the fights ended for good. Over the years, earthquakes, popes, barbarians, and the environment have all played a role in the Colosseum's decay. The pockmarks that riddle the travertine walls indicate where metal-hungry Lombards gouged into the stone in the 9th century to extract the lead fasteners between the blocks. ⏱ *45 min.; crowded until late afternoon—buy tickets at the Roman Forum or Palatine Hill to skip the queue. Piazza del Colosseo.* ☎ *06-7005469. 11€ (includes Roman Forum and Palatine). Daily 9am–1 hr. before sunset. Metro: Colosseo. Bus: 60, 75, 85, 87, 95, or 175. Tram: 3.*

⓫ ★★ **Domus Aurea.** The maniacal emperor Nero snatched up most of the city land that burned in the catastrophic fire of A.D. 64 and built himself a palace that extended from the Palatine to the Oppian Hill, where the underground ruins of the "Golden House" can now be visited. See p 46, bullet ❷.

⓬ ★ **Circo Massimo.** Before there was Russell Crowe in *Gladiator,* there was Charlton Heston in *Ben-Hur.* In the world of ancient Roman sports, it was the chariot races at the Circus Maximus that held fans—300,000 of them—most in thrall. *Metro: Circo Massimo. Bus: 30, 60, 75, or 95. Tram: 3.*

⓭ ★★ **Terme di Caracalla.** Luxurious bathing complexes, like those built by Caracalla in A.D. 212 below the Aventine Hill, were a sort of country club in ancient times, but open to rich and poor, and as integral to the Romans' daily life as shuffling through the Forum on business or watching gladiators slug it out in the Colosseum. ⏱ *45 min. Viale delle Terme di Caracalla 52.* ☎ *06-39967700. 6€. Tues–Sun 9am–1 hr. before sunset, Mon 9am–2pm. Metro: Circo Massimo. Bus:118. Tram: 3.*

The Baths of Caracalla were among the grandest imperial baths in ancient Rome.

The Best **Museums**

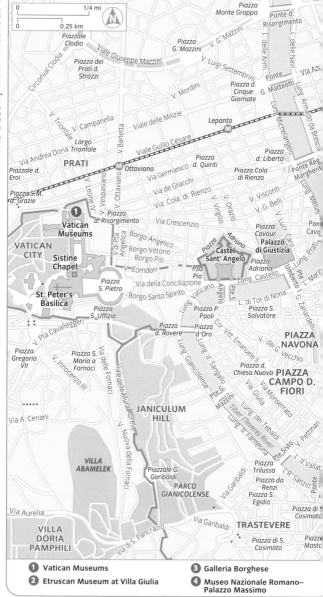

1 Vatican Museums

2 Etruscan Museum at Villa Giulia

3 Galleria Borghese

4 Museo Nazionale Romano–
Palazzo Massimo

⑤ Galleria Doria Pamphilj

⑥ Capitoline Museum

⑦ Terrazza Caffarelli

⑧ Museo della Civiltà Romana

Of the more than 100 museums in Rome, those listed here are my favorites for all-around interest, from intimate family collections to Fascist-era didactic museums. START: Take bus 23, 49, or 492 to the entrance of the Vatican Museums, or take tram 19 to Piazza Risorgimento, or take Metro Line A to Ottaviano-San Pietro or Cipro-Musei Vaticani, and walk.

① ★★★ Vatican Museums. From mummies to moon rocks, the papal collections have the best of everything. See p 49, bullet **⑥**.

② ★★ Etruscan Museum at Villa Giulia. Pope Julius III's gorgeous Mannerist villa houses priceless artifacts, including intricate gold jewelry and a charming his-and-hers sarcophagus, from the civilization that ruled Italy before the Romans. ⏰ *45 min. Piazza Villa Giulia (at Viale delle Belle Arti).* ☎ *06-3226571. 4€. Tues–Sun 9am–7pm. Tram: 2, 3, or 19.*

③ ★★★ Galleria Borghese. Immensely entertaining and mercifully manageable in size, the collection at this 17th-century garden estate is museum perfection. Ancient Roman mosaics in the entrance salon depict gory scenes between gladiators and wild animals. In Room 1, Canova's *Pauline Bonaparte* (1805–08) lies, topless, on a marble divan. Bernini's staggeringly skillful sculptures of *David,*

Apollo and Daphne, and *Rape of Persephone* (1621–24), in Rooms 2 to 4, are so realistically rendered that their subjects seem to be breathing. The paintings by Caravaggio in Room 8 range in tone from luscious (*Boy with a Basket of Fruit,* 1594) to strident and grisly (*David and Goliath,* 1610). Renaissance masterpieces like Raphael's *Deposition* (1507) and Titian's *Sacred and Profane Love* (1514) hang casually upstairs in the *pinacoteca.* ⏰ *1 hr. Piazzale Scipione Borghese.* ☎ *06-32810. www.galleriaborghese.it. Reservations required. 8.50€. Tues–Sun 9am–7pm. Bus: 116 or 910.*

④ ★★ Museo Nazionale Romano—Palazzo Massimo. An embarrassment of ancient riches—paintings, mosaics, statues, and inscriptions—is displayed at this recently restored, bright, and airy palazzo near the train station. Frescoes teeming with delightful animal and vegetable motifs, rescued from the bedrooms and dining

A close-up of Michelangelo's Sistine Chapel ceiling fresco depicts God reaching out to Adam.

The Capitoline Museums lie on the perfectly proportioned Piazza del Campidoglio.

rooms of Roman villas, are the highlight here, and totally unique among Rome's museums. 🕐 *1 hr. Largo di Villa Peretti 1 (at Via Giolitti).* ☎ *06-48903501. 6.50€. Tues–Sun 9am–7pm. Metro: Termini. Bus: 40, 64, 70, 170, 175, or 492.*

⑤ ★★ Galleria Doria Pamphilj. The patinated halls of this noble palace still smell like the 17th century. Masterpieces collected by the Doria Pamphilj family—one of the most influential in Roman history—include works by Caravaggio, Guercino, Raphael, and Titian, and Velázquez's famous portrait of Pope Innocent X Pamphilj. Admission includes the highly entertaining audio tour, narrated by the living princes themselves. 🕐 *1 hr. Via del Corso 305.* ☎ *06-6797323. 8€. Fri–Wed 10am–5pm. Bus: 30, 40, 62, 64, 70, 85, 87, 95, 170, or 492.*

⑥ ★★★ Capitoline Museums (Musei Capitolini). In the Michelangelo-designed buildings of Piazza del Campidoglio are some of the most important Roman sculptures in the world. The Palazzo dei Conservatori houses the 5th-century-B.C. bronze *Capitoline She-wolf,* mascot of Rome, in Room 4, and the photogenic fragments of the colossal statue of *Constantine* in the courtyard. The *pinacoteca* has a number of fine works by Caravaggio, Titian, Tintoretto, and Guido Reni. Across the square in the

Palazzo Nuovo are the majestic 2nd-century-A.D. bronze of *Marcus Aurelius,* haunting busts of emperors and philosophers in Rooms 4 and 5, and myriad marble fauns and satyrs throughout. Not to be missed, the ponderous tufa blocks of the *tabularium* (Roman archive hall, 78 B.C.) connect the two wings of the museums and offer dramatic views over the Forum. 🕐 *1½ hr. Best in late afternoon. Piazza del Campidoglio.* ☎ *06-67102071. 6.50€. Tues–Sun 9am–8pm. Bus: 30, 40, 62, 64, 70, 87, 95, 170, or 492.*

⑦ ★ Terrazza Caffarelli. The Capitoline Museum's cafe has fresh sandwiches and drinks—and a commanding view of the *centro storico.* Non-museumgoers can access the cafe from the northern wall of Palazzo dei Conservatori. *$–$$.*

⑧ ★★ Museo della Civiltà Romana. It's worth the subway ride to Mussolini's fantasyland—EUR—to see the enormous, 1:250-scale plastic model of ancient Rome. The rest of the museum is filled with reproductions of ancient structures (the aqueducts) and fascinating engineering feats (construction of the Colosseum). *Piazza Agnelli 10.* ☎ *06-5926135. 6.50€. Tues–Fri 9am–2pm; Sat–Sun 9am–7pm. Metro: Fermi.*

Baroque Rome

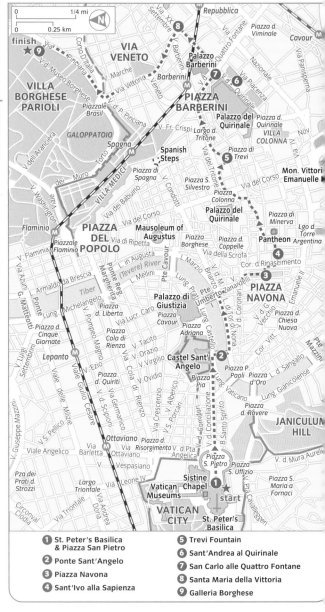

1. St. Peter's Basilica & Piazza San Pietro
2. Ponte Sant'Angelo
3. Piazza Navona
4. Sant'Ivo alla Sapienza
5. Trevi Fountain
6. Sant'Andrea al Quirinale
7. San Carlo alle Quattro Fontane
8. Santa Maria della Vittoria
9. Galleria Borghese

Straight lines and right angles? Ugh—so 1500s! The 17th century in Rome saw a boom in artistic patronage—the biggest in the city since the days of the Caesars—that heralded the arrival of a new style, called *barocco* ("irregular pearl"), in which sculptors and architects traded the balance and symmetry of the Renaissance for dynamism and theatrical flourish. The two greatest exponents of Roman baroque were Francesco Borromini and Gian Lorenzo Bernini, who left their respective curricula vitae virtually strewn about the city. Occasionally over-the-top, but always fun, the baroque style is what gave Rome its signature sinuous building facades and its myriad playful fountains. It's what makes an aimless stroll through the *centro storico* so rewarding. START: **Take bus 23, 40, 62, or 64 to Piazza Pia/Via della Conciliazione.**

① ★★★ **St. Peter's Basilica & Piazza San Pietro.** Reaching out from either side of the church, the curving, colonnaded arms of Piazza San Pietro were designed by Bernini in the 1640s to mimic a gigantic human embrace, clutching visitors, caliper-like, inexorably toward the bosom of St. Peter's Basilica. Under the dome, Bernini's corkscrew-legged bronze baldacchino is flecked with tiny bumblebees, the symbol of his—and the baroque's—greatest patron, Pope Urban VIII Barberini. See p 48, bullets **①** and **②**.

② ★★ **Ponte Sant'Angelo.** The angels studding this bridge to Castel Sant'Angelo are copies of original sculptures by Bernini. Each figure holds an instrument of the passion

This angel is a copy of one of Bernini's original sculptures atop Ponte Sant'Angelo.

Ponte Sant'Angelo, with Castel Sant'Angelo in the background.

of Christ; their masterfully rendered emotions run the gamut from introverted sorrow to wrenching pain to that Bernini warhorse, the parted-lips swoon. ⏱ *15 min. Best at night. Between Castel Sant' Angelo and Lungotevere Sant'Angelo. Bus: 40, 62, or 64.*

③ ★★★ Piazza Navona.

Rome's grandest baroque square is the stage for an architectural smackdown between Borromini and Bernini. Weighing in on the western side of the oblong piazza is Borromini's **Sant'Agnese in Agone** (1653–57), a small church whose proud bearing is enhanced by its telescoping bell towers, oversized dome, and concave facade—a popular baroque feature, designed to draw in passers-by. A bare basin for centuries, the **Fountain of Neptune** was only given its namesake figure and fanciful decoration in the 1800s. In the center, Neptune engages an octopus in fierce battle as unfazed duos of seahorses, nymphs, and aquatic cherubs cavort around the fountain's edge. In the center of the square, Bernini's action-packed, obelisk-crowned **Fountain of the Four Rivers** (1651; see chapter-opening photo) is a feisty competitor, with four

reclining figures representing the Danube, Plata, Ganges, and Nile. The fountain's base is a mass of travertine, hewn in the pre-weathered, organic style so favored in the 17th and 18th centuries. And any baroque sculptor worth his salt would sooner be caught dead than design a fountain that didn't include cavorting animals—today, over-heated tourists and mentally unstable locals splash (illegally) alongside Bernini's "hippopotamus" (which is just a horse wading) and river serpents. Between Borromini and Bernini, who wins? After 350 years, the jury is still out—but if you look up at the left bell tower of the church, a devastatingly *superb* statue of St. Agnes, placed there after the fountain's completion, seems to have the last laugh. *See also p 53, bullet* ⑥.

④ ★ Sant'Ivo alla Sapienza.

Borromini always created drama in his architecture by employing elements of curvaceous tension; here, an upside-down marble tornado of a dome crowns a dizzying, star-shaped church. ⏱ *15 min. Corso Rinascimento 40. Interior open only Sun 9am–noon. Bus: 30, 40, 62, 64, 70, 87, 116, or 492.*

The Fontana del Nettuno (Fountain of Neptune) in Piazza Navona.

Sleeping Hermaphrodite sculpture in the Galleria Borghese.

⑤ ★★★ Trevi Fountain. The tourist swarms are annoying, but Nicola Salvi's fountain (1732–62) is a monumental feast for the eyes that never fails to delight—and to surprise, given its hidden location. An ingeniously sculpted base of faux boulders and "fallen" building cornices gives rise to a dynamic pageant of mythological figures, over which thousands of gallons of water per minute thunder to the inviting blue pool below. ⏱ *30 min. Piazza di Trevi. Crowded from 10am–midnight. Bus: 62, 95, 116, 175, or 492.*

⑥ ★ Sant'Andrea al Quirinale. The smallest church Bernini designed, known as the "pearl of the baroque," is understated only in size. Amid a rich dessert of pink marble and gilded stucco, a plaster St. Andrew steals the show, rising to the heavens past the broken pediment above the altar. ⏱ *15 min. Via del Quirinale 29. Metro: Barberini. Bus: 40, 64, 70, 170, or H.*

⑦ ★★ San Carlo alle Quattro Fontane. It feels almost like being trapped inside an elaborate crystal in Borromini's tiny church (his favorite). This is an oppressive, colorless frenzy of concave chapels, jutting cornices, intricate coffers, and tricks of light. ⏱ *15 min. Via del Quirinale 23. Metro: Barberini. Bus: 40, 62, 64, 70, 95, 116, 170, 175, or 492.*

⑧ ★★ Santa Maria della Vittoria. Still risqué after all these years, Bernini's *Ecstasy of St. Teresa* (in the Cornaro Chapel, to the left of the altar) captures the mystical saint in a moment of spiritual rapture that looks for all the world like another kind of climax. From their "box seat" to the side, the animated Cornaro family members react to the ambiguously scandalous spectacle. ⏱ *15 min. Via XX Settembre 17. Metro: Repubblica. Bus: 60, 62, or 910.*

⑨ ★★★ Galleria Borghese. The word "incredible" is often used lightly, but Bernini's chisel wizardry here truly confounds belief. In his sculptures of *Apollo and Daphne,* *Rape of Persephone,* and *David,* he defies the physical properties of marble, involving us emotionally with his subjects and reverentially with his skill. The museum's strict reservations policy keeps crowds to a blessed minimum; be sure to book at least a few days in advance. *See p 30, bullet* ❸.

Bernini's Ecstasy of St. Teresa *in Santa Maria della Vittoria.*

Rome's Best **Piazzas**

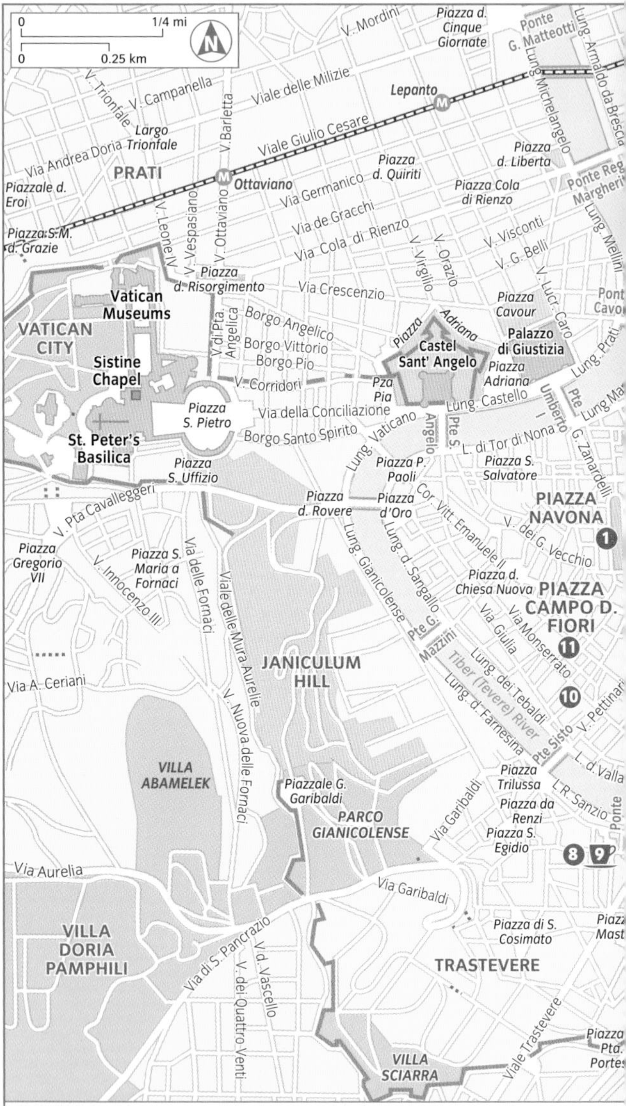

1 Piazza Navona
2 Piazza della Rotonda
3 Piazza San Lorenzo in Lucina
4 Piazza del Popolo
5 D'Angelo
6 Piazza di Spagna

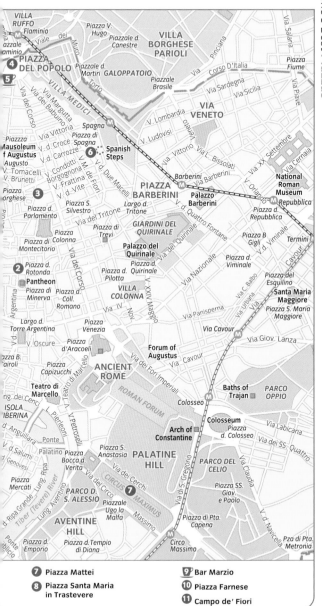

VILLA RUFFO
Flaminio
azzale
aminio

Viale dei Muro

PIAZZA DEL POPOLO ❹
❺

VILLA MEDICI

Via del Corso
Via di Babuino
Via Margutta

Piazza V. Hugo
Piazzale d. Canestre

VILLA BORGHESE PARIOLI

Piazzale d. Martiri GALOPPATOIO

Pinciana

Piazza Fiume

Corso D'Italia

Piazzale Brasile

Via Sardegna

Via Salaria

Via Sicilia

Via Plave

Via Lombardia

VIA VENETO

Via Vittorio Veneto

Via Vittorio
Via L. Bissolati

Via XX Settembre

Via Cernaia

National Roman Museum

Via Ludovisi

Spagna

Piazza di Spagna

Spanish Steps ❻

V. d. Croce
V.d. Carrozze
Via Vittoria

Piazza
Mausoleum
f Augusto

V. Tomacelli
V. Brunetti

Condotti
Borgognona
V. Frattina
V. d. Vite

Piazza
orghese ❸

Piazza d. Parlamento

Piazza di Montecitorio

Piazza Rotonda ❷
Pantheon

Piazza di Minerva

Largo d. Torre Argentina

V. d. Due Macelli

Piazza S. Silvestro

Via del Tritone

Largo d. Tritone

Piazza di Trevi

Piazza d. Pilotta

VILLA COLONNA

Piazza Coll. Romano

Via IV. Nov

PIAZZA BARBERINI

Barberini

Palazzo Barberini

GIARDINI DEL QUIRINALE

Palazzo del Quirinale

Piazza d. Quirinale

Via Barberini

V. d Quattro Fontane

V. Orlando

Piazza d. Repubblica

Repubblica

Piazza d. Viminale

Piazza B Gigli

Via Nazionale

Piazza del Esquilino

Santa Maria Maggiore

Piazza S. Maria Maggiore

Termini

Via Cavour

Via Cernaia

V.d. Viminale

Cavour

Via C. Balbo

Via Urbana

Via Panisperna

Via Giov. Lanza

Piazza Venezia

Piazza d'Aracoeli

Piazza Capizucchi

ANCIENT ROME

Forum of Augustus

Via dei Fori Imperiali

Via Cavour

Colosseo

Baths of Trajan

PARCO OPPIO

Via Labicana

Colosseum

Piazza d. Colosseo

Via dei SS. Quattro

azza B. airoli

Teatro di Marcello

ng. dei Cenci

ISOLA TIBERINA

d. Anguillara

V. d Salumi
. Genovesi

Piazza Mercati

Ponte blico

V. Teatro di Marcello

L. Pierleoni

V. Petroselli

Palatino

Lung. Ripa

d. Ripa Grande

Lung.

Tiber (Tevere) River

ROMAN FORUM

Arch of Constantine

Piazza S. Anastasia

Piazza Bocca d. Verita

Via dei Cerchi

CIRCUS MAXIMUS

PARCO D. S. ALESSIO

AVENTINE HILL

Piazza d. Emporio

Piazza d. Tempio di Diana

PALATINE HILL

Piazzale Ugo la Malfa ❼

Massimo

Via di S. Gregorio

PARCO DEL CELIO

Piazza SS. Giov. e Paolo

Via Claudia

Piazza di Pta. Capena

Circo Massimo

v. d. Navicella

Pza di Pta. Metronia

---

❼ Piazza Mattei

❽ Piazza Santa Maria in Trastevere

❾ Bar Marzio

❿ Piazza Farnese

⓫ Campo de' Fiori

Giving every city neighborhood its own alfresco salon, with newsstands, cafes, and room to breathe, the piazza is one of the great Italian urban inventions. In Rome, some are grandiose gifts to the city from politically minded popes; others are the incidental result of streets meeting at odd angles; but the best piazzas are those where Romans act out their daily pageants, fully aware of their dramatic backdrops. START: **Take bus 30, 40, 62, 64, 70, 87, 116, or 492 to Corso Vittorio Emanuele or Corso Rinascimento.**

1 ★★★ **Piazza Navona.** This theatrical baroque platter retains the shape of the ancient stadium over which it was built. Vying for your attention at the center of the oval are Bernini's dynamic Fountain of the Four Rivers and Borromini's haughty Church of Sant'Agnese in Agone. Cafes and restaurants abound on the square, but you'll never find locals dining here. Piazza Navona is at its best before 10am, when the tourist hordes and trinket sellers start to descend, so come for a morning cappuccino to enjoy an unspoiled view. See p 53, bullet **6**. *Bus: 30, 40, 62, 64, 70, 87, 116, or 492.*

2 ★★★ **Piazza della Rotonda.** Despite a 9m (30-ft.) rise from the surrounding ground level, the 2nd-century-A.D. Pantheon still stands,

The pink granite obelisk in Piazza del Popolo.

awesomely imposing, at the southern end of this square; the fountain is from the 18th century. Stop by in the late evening for a drink, when the atmosphere is more intimate and tourist-free. *Bus: 30, 40, 62, 64, 70, 85, 87, 95, 116, or 175. Tram: 8.*

3 ★ **Piazza San Lorenzo in Lucina.** Tourists have taken over Piazza di Spagna, but well-heeled locals in the Tridente shopping district still have this wedge-shaped square when they want to sit down for Campari and sandwiches. The two cafes here—Ciampini and Teichner—are almost identical, and great for watching big-spending Romans on parade. *Metro: Spagna. Bus: 62, 85, 95, 175, or 492.*

4 ★★ **Piazza del Popolo.** A 4,000-year-old pink granite obelisk with wonderful hieroglyphics presides over this grand, pedestrianized expanse at the top of the Tridente. On the north side of the piazza, Santa Maria del Popolo (p 61, bullet **2**) is a trove of art treasures. *Metro: Flaminio.*

5 ★ **D'Angelo.** This old-fashioned coffee bar, offering pastries and light snacks, has an elegant feel and parlor-style seating (which costs a bit more than counter service). *Via della Croce 30.* ☎ 06-6782556. *$–$$.*

6 ★★ **Piazza di Spagna.** Sure, it's a zoo, but the thousands of tourists and flashy locals who flood this gorgeous square—framed by the Spanish Steps, palm trees, brightly colored *palazzi*, and designer shops galore—must be onto something, right? *Metro: Spagna.*

7 ★ **Piazza Mattei.** A scrappy little square in the old Jewish ghetto charms all with its endearing *Fontana delle Tartarughe* (Fountain of the Tortoises), begun in 1588 by Giacomo della Porta and Taddeo Landini and given its namesake amphibians by Bernini in 1638. *Bus: 23, 30, 40, 62, 63, 64, 70, 87, 170, 280, or 492.*

8 ★★ **Piazza Santa Maria in Trastevere.** The crossroads of daily life in village-y Trastevere meet all criteria: a sprinkling of cafes and restaurants, children with *nonna* in tow, a graceful fountain, and a big church. *Bus: H, 23, 280, or 780. Tram: 8.*

9 ★ **Bar Marzio.** The outdoor tables here offer a prime view across the square to the splendid facade of Santa Maria in Trastevere. *Piazza Santa Maria in Trastevere 15.* ☎ *06-5816095. $*

10 ★★ **Piazza Farnese.** Just steps away from the buzz of the Campo, Piazza Farnese is elegant, sedate, and open, graced on its west side by the stately Palazzo Farnese,

Trastevere is full of colorful sights, like these green shutters set against a rust-red facade.

designed in part by Michelangelo and now home to the French embassy. The fountains here are granite bathtubs filched from the Baths of Caracalla in the 1500s and topped by the Farnese family emblem, the iris. *Bus: 23, 30, 40, 62, 64, 70, 87, 116, 280, or 492. Tram: 8.*

11 ★★★ **Campo de' Fiori.** With a produce market in the morning and a booming social scene at its many bars in the evening, this former "Field of Flowers" is the liveliest square in the *centro storico*. The Campo may lack the architectural refinement of other Roman piazzas, but its round-the-clock utility and heavy traffic of locals are tough to beat. *Bus: 30, 40, 62, 64, 70, 87, 116, or 492. Tram: 8.*

The bustling Campo de' Fiori.

Rome's Best **Churches**

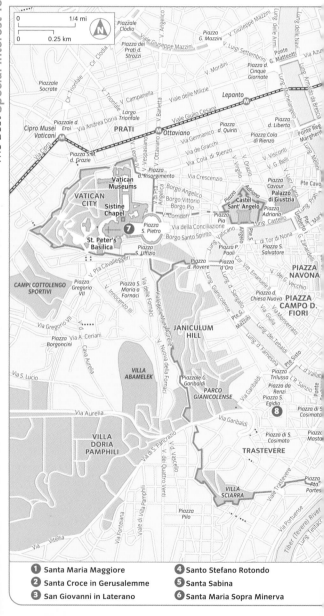

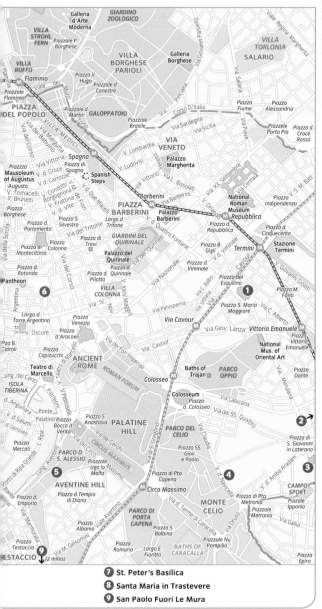

The city's best all-around churches have artistic treasures, relics, and fascinating histories, as well as architecture—humbling or haunting—that reinforce the religious function of the space. All churches in Rome are free of charge and refreshingly cool in summer, but opening hours are notoriously subject to change. START: Take bus 70 or 75 to Piazza Santa Maria Maggiore, or take Metro Line A or B, or bus 40, 64, 170, 175, 492, or H to Stazione Termini, and walk.

① ★★ Santa Maria Maggiore. In this perfect example of the proto-typical basilica, the main nave, flanked by two lower and narrower side aisles, terminates in a curved apse, which is decorated with dazzling polychrome and gold mosaics. Near the right side of the main altar, a modest marble slab marks the tomb of baroque superstar Gian Lorenzo Bernini; the epitaph, inlaid in bronze, is a pithy summary of his life: "He decorated the city." *Piazza di Santa Maria Maggiore.* ☎ *06-483195. Daily 7am–7pm. Metro: Termini. Bus: 70, 75, 649, or 714.*

② ★ Santa Croce in Gerusalemme. The mother lode of relics here includes a piece of the True Cross, remnants of the Crown of Thorns, and the finger of doubting St. Thomas. (Photos aren't allowed, but postcards of all can be purchased at the church gift shop.) *Piazza di Santa Croce in Gerusalemme 12.* ☎ *06-7014769. Metro: Manzoni. Bus: 81 or 649. Tram: 3.*

③ ★★ San Giovanni in Laterano. The cathedral of Rome and mother church of the world is not St. Peter's in the Vatican, but this church dedicated to St. John. The spare, slightly grave interior is by Borromini (1646); the facade, with its chorus line of saints, dates from 1735. In a separate building across the piazza are the Scala Santa (holy stairs) and the Sancta Sanctorum ("holy of holies"), boasting rare 13th-century frescoes by Cimabue and relics of furniture from the Last Supper. *Piazza San Giovanni in Laterano.* ☎ *06-69886433. Free admission to church and Scala Santa; 3€ Sancta Sanctorum. Church daily 7am–6:30pm. Scala Santa daily*

Elegant columns adorned with Cosmatesque mosaics are found in San Giovanni in Laterano.

A nun strolls through St. Peter's Square.

ridiculously prudish golden loincloth was added later. *Piazza della Minerva 42.* ☎ *06-6793926. Daily 7am–7pm. Bus: 30, 40, 62, 64, 70, 87, 116, or 492.*

7 ★★★ **St. Peter's Basilica.** The facade is the pompous result of too many architects' tinkerings, but the sublime interior of St. Peter's (built 1506–1626) is astounding, visit after visit. The church is, quite simply, huge. Its vastness plays out in the building's every feature, from the 2m-tall (6-ft.) Latin inscription to the 45-story-high dome, designed by Michelangelo to "crown" the Roman skyline. See p 48, bullet **2**.

Dress Code

St. Peter's has a hard-and-fast dress code that makes no exceptions to the rule: **Men and women in shorts, above-the-knee skirts, or bare shoulders** will not be admitted to the Vatican City basilica. Period.

6:30am–noon, 3–6pm. Sancta Sanctorum Tues, Thurs, Sat 10:30–11:30am, 3:30–4:30pm. Metro: San Giovanni. Bus: 85, 87, or 117. Tram: 3.

4 ★ **Santo Stefano Rotondo.** Deep in the rustic Celio Hill, this ancient church is reminiscent of a railway roundhouse. The walls of the ambulatory are frescoed with R-rated scenes of gruesome martyrdoms. *Via di Santo Stefano Rotondo 7.* ☎ *06-421191. Nov–Mar Mon–Sat 2–4pm, Tues–Sat 9am–1pm; Apr–Oct Mon–Sat 3:30–6pm, Tues–Sat 9am–1pm. Bus: 81.*

5 ★★ **Santa Sabina.** *See p 20, bullet* **3**.

6 ★★ **Santa Maria Sopra Minerva.** The only Gothic church in the city is a soothing contrast to the sometimes-gaudy baroque interiors of many Roman churches. Pointy medieval arches—meant to emphasize heaven—create soaring vaults that are decorated with a cool, blue, starry sky motif. To the right of the main altar is Michelangelo's underwhelming *Christ Carrying the Cross* (1514–20); the

8 ★★ **Santa Maria in Trastevere.** It's best to visit just after Mass has let out, when the basilica is still fragrant with incense. See p 58, bullet **6**.

9 ★★ **San Paolo Fuori Le Mura.** The immense basilica of St. Paul "Outside the Walls" (one of the Vatican's four patriarchal churches) was built over the site of Paul's tomb in A. D. 324 but heavily damaged by fire in the 19th century. It has since been painstakingly restored. The stunning interior features acres of marble paving, endless colonnades, and mosaic portraits of all the popes from Peter to Benedict XVI—and space is running out. *Via Ostiense 186.* ☎ *06-69880800. Daily 7am–7pm. Metro: Basilica San Paolo. Bus: 23 or 271.*

Romantic Rome

1. Laghetto di Villa Borghese
2. Casina Valadier
3. Pincio
4. Roof Bar at Raphael Hotel
5. Ponte Sant'Angelo
6. Gianicolo
7. Campidoglio

etween gorgeous lookouts, intimate piazzas, panoramic bars, and the general ardor of the natives, Rome is one sprawling romantic setting. Against your best defenses, the itinerary below will have you waxing sappy and gushing *"Ti amo"* from dusk till dawn. START: **Take bus 490 or 495 to Villa Borghese/Viale Fiorello La Guardia, or tram 3 or 19 to Villa Borghese/Viale delle Belle Arti, or bus 52, 53, or 116 to Via Veneto/Piazza San Paolo del Brasile, and walk.**

1 ★ Laghetto di Villa Borghese. Take your lover for a gentle row around Villa Borghese's idyllic lake, which is surrounded by trees and faux temples. Boats can be rented daily from 9:30am to sunset. *Bus: 116, 490, or 495. Tram: 3 or 19.*

2 ★★ Casina Valadier. Toast the sweetness of life at the garden cafe/bar of the fancy Casina Valadier restaurant. *Piazza Bucarest.* ☎ 06-69922090. *Metro: Spagna.* $$–$$$.

3 ★★★ Pincio. The utterly tryst-worthy Pincio gardens have secluded corners, umbrella pine bowers, and spectacular stone balustrades overlooking the rooftops of the *centro* and across to St. Peter's. Recommended during the

The roof bar at the Raphael Hotel.

lingering glow after sunset, or in the full dark of night. *Metro: Flaminio.*

4 ★★ Roof Bar at Raphael Hotel. After dinner, stroll over to this Piazza Navona–area hotel, whose romantic rooftop is perfect for a post-meal *digestivo*. *Largo Febo 2.* ☎ 06- 682831. *Bus: 30, 70, 87, 116, or 492.* $$$.

5 ★★★ Ponte Sant'Angelo. The bridge, lined with Bernini angels, is featured in many hot-and-heavy Italian TV commercials and movie scenes, if that tells you anything. It's especially bewitching by night. *Bus: 30, 40, 62, 64, or 571.*

6 ★★ Gianicolo. No romantic Roman itinerary is complete without the city's make-out point par excellence, the Janiculum Hill. The tree-lined ridge above Trastevere is perfect for a lovers' stroll, with comprehensive panoramas that span the *centro* from St. Peter's to the Baths of Caracalla. *Piazza Garibaldi/Passeggiata del Gianicolo. Bus: 115 or 870.*

7 ★★★ Campidoglio. The sublime, deserted piazza is a fine place to be at night in romantic company, but the evening view from the Campidoglio terraces over the Roman Forum, where floodlit marble columns and arches recede majestically into the dark valley toward the ghosts of the ancients, is quite possibly the most rapturous sight in the world. *Bus: 30, 40, 62, 64, 70, 87, 95, 116, 170, or 492.*

Underground Rome

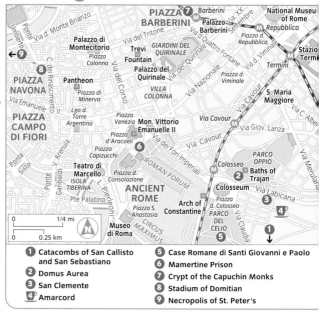

1 Catacombs of San Callisto and San Sebastiano
2 Domus Aurea
3 San Clemente
4 Amarcord
5 Case Romane di Santi Giovanni e Paolo
6 Mamertine Prison
7 Crypt of the Capuchin Monks
8 Stadium of Domitian
9 Necropolis of St. Peter's

In a city whose street level has risen about 9m (30 ft.) (due to flooding of the Tiber) since the days of the Caesars, it's only natural that a whole other Rome should exist hidden away beneath the modern buildings. The catacombs have been drawing visitors underground for centuries, but there are also plenty of places (some newly opened) within the city center that permit visitors a fascinating descent into the bowels of history. START: **Take bus 118 or a taxi to the Catacombs of San Callisto or San Sebastiano, on the Via Appia Antica.**

1 ★★ **Catacombs of San Callisto and San Sebastiano.** Rome's most famous underground tourist attractions, the catacombs, are outside the city walls, as ancient Roman law forbade burials within the sacred *pomerium*, or city boundary. Of Rome's 65 known catacombs—networks of hand-dug tunnels that became massive "dormitories" for the dead—only a handful are open to the public. The catacombs of San Callisto are the largest, with 500,000 burial niches (*loculi*). Nearby, the catacombs of San Sebastiano are more intimate. See p 95.

2 ★★ **Domus Aurea.** The cavernous halls of nutty Nero's former pad feature nymphaeums (ornamental grottoes built as shrines to water nymphs) with fake stalactites, rooms frescoed in the *grotesque* (grotto-esque) style, and the famed octagonal dining room. 🕐 *45 min. Via della Domus Aurea.* 📞 *06-39967700. Reservations required. 6.50€. Wed–Mon*

9am–7:45pm. Metro: Colosseo. Bus: 60, 75, 85, 87, 95, or 175. Tram: 3.

3 ★★ **San Clemente.** This "lasagna of churches" is the best place in Rome to understand the city's archaeological evolution. Descend 18m (60 ft.) through medieval and paleo-Christian layers to the lowest level, where adherents of the ancient cult of Mithras met and performed grisly rituals in the long, rectangular *mithraeum.* ◔ *30 min. Via di San Giovanni in Laterano.* ☎ *06-70451018. 5€. Mon–Sat 9am–12:30pm, 3–6pm; Sun 10am–12:30pm, 3–6pm. Metro: Colosseo. Bus: 60, 75, 85, 87, 95, or 175. Tram: 3.*

4 ★ **Amarcord.** Pick up a custom-made *piadina* (flatbread sandwich, a specialty of Fellini's native Rimini) and soft drink or beer at this casual lunch spot frequented by local students and office workers. *Via di San Giovanni in Laterano 164.* ☎ *347-7679342. Closed Sun. $–$$.*

5 ★ **Case Romane di Santi Giovanni e Paolo.** Recent excavations beneath this Romanesque church on the Celio Hill revealed 1st-century-A.D. Roman houses with splendid wall frescoes. ◔ *45 min. Piazza Santi Giovanni e Paolo 13.* ☎ *06-70454544. www.caseromane. it. 6€. Thurs–Mon 10am–1pm, 3–6pm. Metro: Colosseo. Bus: 60, 75, 85, 87, 95, or 175. Tram: 3.*

6 ★ **Mamertine Prison.** Dank and oppressive, these black-rock chambers are said to be where saints Peter and Paul were imprisoned before their martyrdoms. Claustrophobes steer clear. ◔ *15 min. Clivo Argentario 1.* ☎ *06-6792902. Donation expected. Daily 9am–noon, 2:30–5pm. Bus: 60, 85, 87, 95, or 175.*

7 ★★★ **Crypt of the Capuchin Monks.** Macabre yet oddly pleasing, this must-see church crypt is decorated with thousands of artfully arranged monks' bones. Each chapel is a bizarre diorama where propped-up monks, still in their desiccated skin and cassocks, strike cautionary poses. ◔ *20 min. Via Veneto 27.* ☎ *06-4871185. Donation expected. Daily 9am–noon, 3–6pm. Metro: Barberini. Bus: 62, 95, 116, 175, or 492.*

8 ★★ **Stadium of Domitian.** At the northern end of Piazza Navona, explore the fascinating remains of the 1st-century-A.D. athletic venue that gave the square its oblong shape. ◔ *45 min. Piazza di Tor Sanguigna 16.* ☎ *06-67103819. 6€. Sat–Sun 10am–1pm or by appointment. Bus: 70, 87, 116, or 492.*

9 ★★ **Necropolis of St. Peter's.** Positively chill-inducing, these humble, narrow tunnels beneath the immense Vatican basilica make for an unforgettable descent into early Christian history. See p 49, bullet **4**.

The Crypt of the Capuchin Monks.

Vatican City

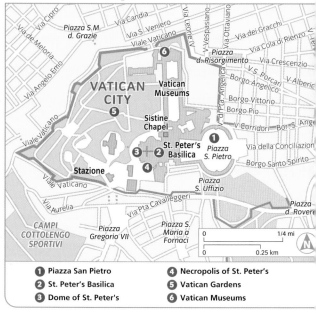

1. Piazza San Pietro
2. St. Peter's Basilica
3. Dome of St. Peter's
4. Necropolis of St. Peter's
5. Vatican Gardens
6. Vatican Museums

Welcome to Popeland, the sovereign state of visual delights. From the star-studded halls of the Vatican Museums to the gargantuan volume of St. Peter's Basilica, the Holy See is brimming with things for the tourist to see and do. Allow about 4 hours to take it in. START: **Take bus 23, 49, or 492 to Viale Vaticano/Viale dei Bastioni di Michelangelo, or take Metro Line A to Ottaviano-San Pietro or Cipro-Musei Vaticani, and walk.**

---

1 ★★★ Piazza San Pietro.
Designed in the 1630s by Bernini to mimic a human embrace, this sweeping colonnade is the gateway to the largest church in the world. In the center stands an Egyptian obelisk that once marked the center of Nero's Circus, where St. Peter was martyred in A.D. 64. Along the south wall of the square are official Vatican souvenir and bookshops and a branch of the Vatican post office. ⏱ *30 min. Free admission.*

2 ★★★ St. Peter's Basilica.
Everything in St. Peter's is made of marble, bronze, or gold, and what appear to be altar paintings are actually mosaics with minuscule *tesserae.* The outstanding artworks in the basilica include Michelangelo's intensely moving *Pietà* (1499) and Bernini's spiral-legged bronze Baldacchino (1633). ⏱ *45 min. Free admission. Daily 7am–7pm; can vary with papal appearances and religious holidays.*

St. Peter's Square and Basilica at night.

3 ★ **Dome of St. Peter's.** Recommended for those who can't visit a European city without climbing a dome—its perspective on the Vatican is impressive, but its general city view is overrated. A coffee bar was opened at the dome's midway point in late 2004. 🕐 *45 min. Queue is shortest in early morning or late afternoon. Piazza San Pietro. 6€ (lift, then stairs); 5€ (all stairs). Daily 9am–5pm.*

4 ★★★ **Necropolis of St. Peter's.** A haunting descent beneath the basilica takes you into the ancient level where bones believed to be St. Peter's were found in the 1940s. See also p 47, bullet **9**. 🕐 *45 min. Ufficio Scavi.* ☎ *06-69885318. Fax 06-69885518. uffscavi@fabricsp.va. 10€. Tours Mon–Sat 9am–5pm. Book at least 1 month in advance.*

5 ★★ **Vatican Gardens.** An oasis of manicured lawns, quaint fountains, and the occasional nun-driven Vespa exists behind the imposing Vatican fortification walls. 🕐 *1 hr.* ☎ *06-69884466. Fax 06-69885100. 10€. Tours Tues, Thurs–Sat 10am only. Book at least 1 week in advance.*

Longer Hours for the Museums & Sistine Chapel

Good news! As of 2008, the Vatican Museums are open Monday to Saturday from 8:30am to 4pm (visitors have to leave by 6pm). This amounts to almost 15 more weekly hours of opening time than the old schedule, which should alleviate some of the crowding problems. I still recommend going in the afternoon—on midweek days like Tuesday or Thursday, you'll have the place to yourself. Before noon is when all the cruise ship groups and package tours descend and the line can take hours to get through.

6 ★★★ **Vatican Museums.** The richest museum in the world is enthralling in its quantity and quality, aggravating in its utter lack of explanatory signage. As a rule, the important stuff is where the crowds are, but try to resist the riptide of tour groups that washes headlong toward the Sistine Chapel, skipping a ton of fabulous art along the way. The museum guidebook—or, better yet, the CD-ROM audio-guide—can make your meander through these masterpiece-packed halls vastly more meaningful. (The Museums' website, **http://mv.vatican.va**, is also an excellent source of background information.)

Start your tour of the Museums in the ★★ **Pinacoteca** (picture gallery), home to Raphael's *Transfiguration* (1520; his last painting), in Room 8; Leonardo's enigmatic *St. Jerome* (1482), in Room 9; and Caravaggio's eerie, green-fleshed *Deposition* (1604), in Room 12. In the Octagonal Courtyard (part of the Pio-Clementine museums of classical statuary), the exquisite marble ★★ **Apollo Belvedere** (a 2nd-c.-A.D. copy of a 5th-c. B.C. original) is a paragon of classical composure. In radical stylistic contrast, the stunning 1st-century-A.D. ★★★ **Laocoon** (Lay-*ah*-koh-on) captures the very height of human vulnerability. The sculpture depicts the fate of a Trojan priest who was suspicious of the Trojan horse and asked his people to "beware of Greeks bearing gifts." The Greek-favoring gods, angered, sentenced him to death by sea serpents. The expressive, though fragmentary, ★ **Belvedere Torso** inspired Michelangelo's rendering of Christ in the *Last Judgment,* in the Sistine Chapel. Upstairs, the ★ **Etruscan Museum** has knockout gold breastplates from a 2,500-year- old

The Laocoon sculpture in the Vatican Museums is from the 1st century A.D.

tomb. From here, the Vatican Museums morph into fresco heaven.

The brightly colored frescoes in the ★ **Gallery of the Maps** are a wonderfully detailed cartographical record of 16th-century Italy. Pink-tinged frescoes by Giulio Romano in the ★ **Hall of Constantine** (1522–25) are a tribute to Christianity toppling paganism. In the famed ★★★ **Raphael Rooms** (1506–17), exquisite frescoes like *School of Athens* and *Liberation of St. Peter* display the harmony of color and balance of composition that were the hallmark of High Renaissance classicism and Raphael's mastery.

After the Raphael Rooms, a wrong turn and confusing signs can take you downstairs to the Vatican's dreadful modern art collection; stay to the left for the direct route to the ★★★ **Sistine Chapel,** where Michelangelo's spectacular frescoes very much live up to the hype, and after a restoration in the 1980s and '90s, they're more eye-popping than ever. On the ceiling (1508–12), the stories of creation, Adam and Eve, and Noah are told in nine frames, surrounded by faux architectural elements and medallions. On the altar wall, the swirling *Last Judgment* (1535–41) is much more fire-and-brimstone, reflecting the anger and disappointment of Michelangelo's later years. Exit the museums via the right rear door of the Sistine Chapel to go straight to St. Peter's. Exit via the left door to return any rented audioguides. 🕐 *2 hr. Go after 12:30pm in high season. Viale Vaticano.* ☎ *06-69883333. http://mv.vatican.va. 14€ adults, 8€ students. Audioguide 6€. Mon–Sat 8:30am–4pm (exit by 6pm). Last Sun of month open 8:30am–12:30pm (exit by 2pm). Closed Catholic holidays—check website for most up-to-date schedule.* ●

Piazza Navona & the Pantheon

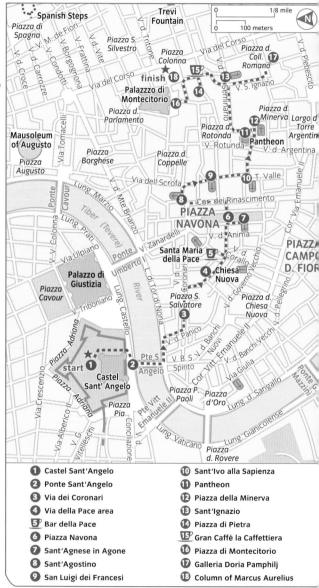

0 ——— 1/8 mile
0 ——— 100 meters
N

Spanish Steps
Piazza di Spagna
Trevi Fountain
Piazza S. Silvestro
Piazza Colonna
Piazza d. Coll. Romano
finish
Palazzzo di Montecitorio
Piazza d. Parlamento
Piazza d. Minerva
Piazza d. Rotonda
Pantheon
Largo d Torre Argentin
Mausoleum of Augusto
Piazza Augusto
Piazza Borghese
Piazza d. Coppelle
V. Rotunda
V. d. Argentina
Via dell Scrofa
Cor. dei Rinascimento
T. Valle
PIAZZA NAVONA
Palazzo di Giustizia
Piazza Cavour
Santa Maria della Pace
Chiesa Nuova
Piazza S. Salvatore
Piazza d. Chiesa Nuova
PIAZZA CAMPO D. FIOR
start
Castel Sant' Angelo
Piazza Pia
Piazza P. Paoli
Piazza d'Oro
Piazza d. Rovere

1 Castel Sant'Angelo
2 Ponte Sant'Angelo
3 Via dei Coronari
4 Via della Pace area
5 Bar della Pace
6 Piazza Navona
7 Sant'Agnese in Agone
8 Sant'Agostino
9 San Luigi dei Francesi
10 Sant'Ivo alla Sapienza
11 Pantheon
12 Piazza della Minerva
13 Sant'Ignazio
14 Piazza di Pietra
15 Gran Caffè la Caffettiera
16 Piazza di Montecitorio
17 Galleria Doria Pamphilj
18 Column of Marcus Aurelius

Previous page: Bicycles are common sights on the streets of Rome.

Prepare to switch sightseeing gears quickly in the most central part of the old city—quiet, labyrinth-like alleys abruptly give way to imposing monuments and knockout postcard panoramas, and a slew of nonchalant-looking churches stash away some of the city's most celebrated works of art. START: **Take bus 40, 62, or 74 to Castel Sant'Angelo/Piazza Pia.**

1 ★★★ Castel Sant'Angelo. Rome's hamburger of history started out as Hadrian's mausoleum in the 2nd century A.D. and was converted in the Middle Ages into a fortress for the popes, who then gave themselves apartments here in the Renaissance. Its final incarnation, as a prison, lasted through the end of the 19th century, long enough to inspire Puccini's *Tosca*. Be sure to climb all the way up to the highest terrace—looking straight down over the Tiber is as soaring and dramatic as an operatic finale. ⏱ *1 hr. Lungotevere Castello 50.* ☎ *06-6819111. 7€. Tues–Sun 9am–7pm.*

2 ★★ Ponte Sant'Angelo. *See p 33, bullet* **2**.

3 ★ Via dei Coronari. This charming little street was formerly a pilgrim route to the Vatican; today, it's lined with antiquarians' shops and intersected by dozens of quaint alleys, with hidden trattorie and artists' studios.

4 ★ Via della Pace area. Via della Pace bisects the web of streets, known as the "triangle of fun," between Via dei Coronari and Via del Governo Vecchio. By day, motorcycle mechanics rub shoulders with Roman nobility; by night, Roman hipsters flock to the area's countless eateries and *boîtes*.

5 ★ Bar della Pace. The chic and the restless flutter in and out of this eternally fashionable cafe from morning to night, but I recommend you stay awhile—it's a prime spot for reading, postcard-writing, and ogling the lovely Santa Maria della Pace, just down the street. *Via della Pace 3–7.* ☎ *06-6861216. $$.*

6 ★★★ Piazza Navona. Nine meters (30 ft.) below the baroque

A close-up view of Ponte Sant'Angelo with Castel Sant'Angelo in the background.

Tourists taking a break in Piazza Navona.

fountains and churches located here is the site where the ancient *agones* (athletic competitions) were held in the Stadium of Domitian (p 47, bullet ⑧). In the medieval period, the Romans called this space *platea in agona* ("place of competition"), which later evolved into the modern appellation, Piazza Navona. See p 53, bullet ❸.

⑦ ★ **Sant'Agnese in Agone.** Borromini's broad, flamboyant facade belies this church's rather small interior. Through a door marked SACRA TESTA, to the left of the altar, there's a reliquary holding the chimpanzee-sized skull of St. Agnes, martyred here in the 4th century A.D. ⏱ *15 min. Piazza Navona. No phone. Free admission. Tues–Sun 9am–noon, 4–7pm.*

⑧ ★ **Sant'Agostino.** On the left wall, Caravaggio's *Madonna dei Pellegrini* (1604) shocked contemporaries with its frank depiction of dirty-footed pilgrims. On a pillar nearby, Raphael's meaty *Isaiah* (1512) recalls the frescoes of the Sistine Chapel. ⏱ *20 min. Piazza Sant'Agostino.* ☎ *06-68801962. Free admission. Daily 8am–noon, 4–7:30pm.*

⑨ ★★ **San Luigi dei Francesi.** Revolutionary for their high-keyed emotions and contrived play of light, Caravaggio's three *Life of St. Matthew* altarpieces (1603), displayed here, are some of his greatest masterpieces. ⏱ *20 min. Piazza San Luigi dei Francesi.* ☎ *06-688271. Free admission. Daily 8:30am–12:30pm; Mon–Wed, Fri–Sun 3:30–7pm.*

⑩ ★★ **Sant'Ivo alla Sapienza.** See p 34, bullet ❹.

⑪ ★★★ **Pantheon.** Hands-down the most masterful architectural feat of ancient Rome, the Pantheon is almost perfectly preserved. The porch consists of 16 monolithic Egyptian granite columns, weighing 74 metric tons (82 tons) each. Inside, the 44m-wide (143-ft.) dome—poured in concrete in the 120s A.D. and never structurally modified—is pierced by a 9m-wide (30-ft.) oculus, open to the sky.

Sunlight streams from the oculus in the dome of the Pantheon.

While most ancient buildings lost their marbles to the popes, the Pantheon's brick walls retain their rich revetment of yellow marble and purple porphyry. The tombs of Raphael and the Savoia monarchs are also here. ⏱ *30 min. Best in early morning or late afternoon, and in the rain. Piazza della Rotonda.* ☎ *06-68300230. Free admission. Daily 9am–6pm, until 7:30pm in summer.*

⑫ ★★ Piazza della Minerva. In front of the Gothic church Santa Maria Sopra Minerva (p 43, bullet ⑥), an Egyptian obelisk—1 of 13 in Rome—is supported on the back of a plucky elephant, sculpted by Bernini. The neighborhood is also home to most of Rome's religious outfitters, with their fabulous window displays of gem-encrusted chalices and the latest in liturgical couture.

⑬ ★ Sant'Ignazio. The focal point of this tight and tidy baroque square is the Jesuit Church of St. Ignatius, famous for its illusionist-style "dome," frescoed on the church's flat roof by Andrea Pozzo in 1626. ⏱ *15 min. Piazza di Sant'Ignazio.* ☎ *06-6794406. Free admission. Daily 7:30am–12:15pm, 4–7pm.*

⑭ ★★ Piazza di Pietra. The impressive row of columns here were the north wall of the 2nd-century-A.D. Temple of Hadrian, a plastic model of which can be seen in a showcase window across the square.

⑮ ★ Gran Caffè La Caffettiera. This elegant coffee and snack bar (and outré Internet hotspot) is especially cozy in winter. Piazza di Pietra 65. ☎ *06-6798147. $–$$.*

⑯ ★ Piazza di Montecitorio. On this sloping square in front of the

The Column of Marcus Aurelius rises from Piazza Colonna.

Bernini-designed lower house of Parliament, dapper *carabinieri* (army police) survey the scene for terrorists—and eligible foreign women. The 2,600-year-old obelisk, moved here in 1751, was the shadow-casting *gnomon* of Augustus's sundial (9 B.C.), an approximation of which is inlaid in bronze over the square.

⑰ ★★ Galleria Doria Pamphilj. This collection, whose audioguide is read (in English) by a living Pamphilj prince, has an enviable array of 16th- and 17th-century canvases, as well as Velázquez's famously soul-exposing portrait of Pope Innocent X Pamphilj. *Piazza del Collegio Romano 2.* ☎ *06-6797323. www. doriapamphilj.it. 8€. Fri–Wed 10am–5pm.*

⑱ ★ Column of Marcus Aurelius. Dismissed by some art historians as a cheap imitation of Trajan's Column (p 24, bullet ⑤), this 30m-high (100-ft.) marble shaft (180–96 A.D.) depicts Marcus Aurelius's military exploits in Germany. *Piazza Colonna.*

Campo de' Fiori

1. Campo de' Fiori
2. Craftsmen's streets
3. Piazza Farnese
4. Via Giulia
5. Galleria Spada
6. Via dei Giubbonari
7. Via di Grotta Pinta
8. Sant'Andrea della Valle
9. Area Sacra di Largo Argentina

Unpretentious, workaday, and totally picturesque, the area around Campo de' Fiori is the best place in the *centro storico* to see Roman daily life at its most authentic. Locals far outnumber tourists, and you can't walk a few steps without coming across a coffee bar, wine shop, or neighborhood trattoria. START: **Take bus 30, 40, 62, 64, 70, 87, 116, 492, 571, or 628 to Corso Vittorio Emanuele, or tram 8 to Largo Argentina, and then walk.**

① ★★★ Campo de' Fiori.

Bustling with energy night and day, and welcoming all, Campo de' Fiori is the beating heart of the *centro storico*. In the morning, the stalls of the city's most famous fruit and vegetable market sell produce to top chefs and local housewives. At night, all and sundry descend on the piazza's cafes and wine bars for the evening *aperitivo*.

② ★★ Craftsmen's Streets.

Many of the streets in the *centro storico* are named for the crafts practiced by artisans there throughout the ages; the best examples of these lie north of the Campo. On Via dei Cappellari, medieval hatmakers have been replaced by furniture workshops, where old men (and some young) make table legs on lathes powered by foot pedals. Off Via del Pellegrino, tiny Arco degli Acetari (Vinegar-Makers' Arch) is the ramshackle, ochre-walled corner featured on so many Roman postcards.

A vendor selling produce in Campo de' Fiori.

3 ★★ Piazza Farnese. Serene Piazza Farnese enjoys the same Renaissance harmony as its namesake architectural feature, the dignified and imposing 16th-century Palazzo Farnese. The square and its immediate vicinity have recently become some of the most sought-after real estate in the city, with fabulous flats that accommodate visiting film stars on location in Rome.

4 ★★ Via Giulia. The dead-straight path of Via Giulia—for many, the most beautiful street in Rome—was cleared by Pope Julius II in the 1500s to give pilgrims a fail-safe passage to the Vatican. The picturesque ivy-covered arch that spans the street was to be part of a private bridge—never completed—for the Farnese family, connecting Palazzo Farnese with the Villa Farnesina, across the river in Trastevere.

5 ★ Galleria Spada. Private galleries with works by Titian and other Renaissance masters are almost a dime a dozen in Rome; what makes the Spada especially worth a visit is the uncannily deceptive Borromini Corridor, which is only 9m (30 ft.) long but appears to be three times that. ⏱ *30 min. Piazza Capo di Ferro 3.* ☎ *06-6874896. 5€. Tues–Sun 9am–7pm. Bus: 23, 30, 40, 62, 64, 70, 87, 116, 280, or 492. Tram: 8.*

6 ★ Via dei Giubbonari. Shopaholics rejoice—this narrow, cobblestone thoroughfare is bursting with up-and-coming fashion boutiques, gourmet food stores, and street vendors.

7 Via di Grotta Pinta. The inward curve of this hidden road, named for the underlying "painted grotto" of the 55 B.C. Theater of Pompey, corresponds with the *cavea* (seating area) of the ancient theater.

8 ★ Sant'Andrea della Valle. The second highest dome in Rome—after St. Peter's—rests atop this excellent 16th-century basilica, where Puccini set the first act of *Tosca.* ⏱ *15 min. Corso Vittorio Emanuele II 6.* ☎ *06-6861339. Free admission. Daily 8am–noon, 4:30–7:30pm.*

9 ★ Area Sacra di Largo Argentina. During the excavation fever of the 1930s, Mussolini evicted hundreds of Romans who were living here and ordered archaeologists to dig. What you see here today, 9m (30 ft.) below street level, are four Republican temple foundations and a much-hyped, though visually underwhelming, fragment of the Senate house (Curia Pompei) where Julius Caesar was stabbed on the Ides of March, 44 B.C. *Ruins open by appointment only.* ☎ *06-67103819. Fax 06-6790795.*

Trastevere

① Vicolo dell'Atleta
② Santa Cecilia
③ San Francesco a Ripa
④ Frontoni
⑤ Via dei Fienaroli
⑥ Piazza Santa Maria in Trastevere
⑦ Via della Scala to Via del Moro
⑧ Panificio la Renella
⑨ Piazza Trilussa
⑩ Caffè Settimiano
⑪ Gianicolo
⑫ Tempietto and San Pietro in Montorio

Separated from the rest of the old city by the river, pictur-esque Trastevere has strived to maintain its own identity since ancient times, when it was dubbed *Trans Tiberim* ("across the Tiber"). Although expatriates have relocated here in droves, the dis-trict still has its insular character and village-y appeal. START: **Take bus 23, 271, 280, 780, H, or tram 8 to Piazza G.G. Belli (Lungotevere degli Anguillara/Viale Trastevere).**

① ★ **Vicolo dell'Atleta.** The "alley of the athlete"—as tiny as streets get in Rome—has a facade of a 13th-century synagogue, now the restaurant Spirito di Vino (p 114).

② ★★ **Santa Cecilia.** See p 15, bullet ①.

③ ★ **San Francesco a Ripa.** Home to Bernini's overtly sexual *Beata Ludovica Albertoni* (1674). ⏱ 15 min. Piazza San Francesco d'Assisi 88. ☎ 06-5819020. Free admis-sion. Daily 7:30am–noon, 4–7pm.

④ ★★ **Frontoni.** Fuel up on pizza-bread sandwiches, stuffed with deli meats, cheeses, or roasted vegeta-bles. *Viale Trastevere 52.* ☎ 06-5812436. $–$$.

⑤ ★ **Via dei Fienaroli.** Dense ivy blankets the walls of this pretty street, hiding numerous interesting bookshops and cafes.

⑥ ★★ **Piazza & Basilica Santa Maria in Trastevere.** The hub of

Wining, dining, and being serenaded in a Trastevere cafe.

daily life in Trastevere is graced by the magnificent church of Santa Maria in Trastevere, with 22 recycled Roman columns lining the nave and sparkling mosaics adorning the apse. Legend has it the church was built over the spot where a fountain of oil miraculously bubbled up in 38 B.C., apparently heralding the coming of Christ. The piazza's handsome fountain, by Carlo Fontana, is somewhat blighted by omnipresent drunks and their flea-bitten dogs. *See p 39, bullet* ⑧*, and p 43, bullet* ⑧.

⑦ ★ **Via della Scala to Via del Moro.** This warren of gnarled streets (Vicolo del Cedro, Vicolo del Bologna, Piazza de' Renzi) is the most charming part of old Trastevere, where clotheslines are strung over narrow alleys, parking jobs reach new heights of ingenuity, and neighbors chat animatedly.

⑧ ★★ **Panificio la Renella.** Purveyor of *pane* to all restaurants and households in the vicinity, this bread bakery also has excellent pizza by the slice, bar stools to sit on, and a community message board. *Via del Moro 15–16.* ☎ *06-5817265. $.*

⑨ **Piazza Trilussa.** This is the point of egress for all the tiny

streets in the area, and where pedestrian Ponte Sisto leads across the Tiber toward Campo de' Fiori.

⑩ ★ **Caffè Settimiano.** In the shadow of the old Septimian Gate (part of the 3rd-c.-A.D. Aurelian Walls), this is a wonderful place to rest your feet, read the paper, and watch *trasteverini* go by. *Via di Porta Settimiana.* ☎ *06-5810468. $.*

⑪ ★★★ **Gianicolo.** The hike to the top of Janiculum Hill—the highest point in central Rome—is steep, but well worth the spectacular views, tree-lined promenades, and clear air. Don't miss the fabulously inviting 17th-century Fontanone dell'Acqua Paola. 🕐 *30 min. Take Via Garibaldi to Via di Porta San Pancrazio and climb the steps to the Passeggiata del Gianicolo.*

⑫ ★ **Tempietto and San Pietro in Montorio.** In the courtyard of this church is Donato Bramante's round, classically inspired Tempietto (1508), one of Rome's greatest, and least visited, architectural masterpieces. 🕐 *15 min. Piazza San Pietro in Montorio 2.* ☎ *06-5813940. Free admission. Tempietto daily 10am–noon, 2–4pm.*

Tridente

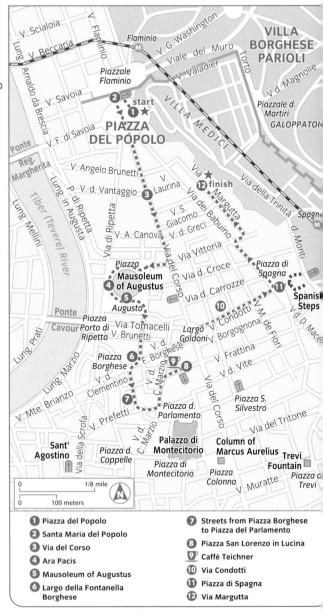

1 Piazza del Popolo
2 Santa Maria del Popolo
3 Via del Corso
4 Ara Pacis
5 Mausoleum of Augustus
6 Largo della Fontanella
   Borghese

7 Streets from Piazza Borghese
   to Piazza del Parlamento
8 Piazza San Lorenzo in Lucina
9 Caffè Teichner
10 Via Condotti
11 Piazza di Spagna
12 Via Margutta

Named for the three-pronged splay of streets (Via Ripetta, Via del Corso, and Via del Babuino) south of Piazza del Popolo, the Tridente is the toniest part of town, where wealthy neighborhood co-ops keep their cobblestone streets swept clean and lined with potted plants. The area east of Via del Corso is a shopper's paradise; to the west, it's darker and quieter, with doglegged alleys that evoke the 16th century. Relieved on both sides by open spaces (the Tiber and the Villa Borghese), the air here is jaunty and glamorous. Note that "Tridente" is a term largely made up for the convenience of guidebook writers; locals usually refer to this neighborhood by its principal streets or squares (Piazza di Spagna and Piazza del Popolo). START: **Take Metro Line A to Flaminio, or take bus 62, 85, 95, 116, 175, or 492 to Largo Chigi, and walk.**

1 ★★★ **Piazza del Popolo.** In the tradition of the grandest Roman piazzas, the vertex of the Tridente is vast, sun-drenched, and obelisked. It was given its present oval shape by neoclassical architect Giuseppe Valadier in 1818 and made traffic-free in 1998. The piazza is bounded to the east by the glorious green terraces of the Pincio gardens, one of the most romantic spots in the city. *See p 38, bullet* **4**.

2 ★★ **Santa Maria del Popolo.** In 1099, a church was built on this spot to "expel the demons"— tradition holds that the detested emperor Nero was secretly buried here by his mistress, Poppaea Sabina, in 68 A.D. The low-ceilinged interior is at first unremarkable, but look closely and you'll find works by Bramante, Pinturicchio, Raphael, and Bernini, as well as two masterpieces by Caravaggio—the tipsy *Martyrdom of St. Peter* (1600) and *Conversion of St. Paul* (1601), with its prominent horse's butt. 🕐 *30 min. Piazza del Popolo 12.* 📞 *06-3610836. Mon–Sat 7am–noon, 4–7pm; Sun 8am–1pm, 4:30–7:30pm.*

3 **Via del Corso.** Named for the barbaric riderless horse races *(corse)* that took place here during *Carnevale,* Via del Corso is the main

A rainbow rises over the rooftops of Piazza del Popolo.

north–south thoroughfare in the *centro storico* and packed with mid-range boutiques. The pedestrianized northern half is the favorite stamping ground of obnoxious Roman teens and best avoided if you're looking for a pleasant place to stroll.

④ ★★ Ara Pacis. Housed in a strikingly modern, Richard Meier–designed pavilion along the river-bank, this 9 B.C. "Altar of Peace" is one of the most important works of Roman relief sculpture in the world. The marble panels making up the square altar depict Emperor Augustus and his entourage and mythological scenes of the deities that supposedly protected Rome and fostered peace within it; the Ara Pacis was commissioned when Augustus returned triumphant from his military endeavors in Gaul and Spain. The museum structure, opened in 2006, is the first work of new architecture in the *centro storico* since the fascist period. ⏲ *30 min. Lungotevere in Augusta.* ☎ *06-82059127. 6.50€. Tues–Sun 9am–7pm.*

The Valentino shop on stylish Via Condotti.

⑤ ★ Mausoleum of Augustus. This crumbling though still massive brick cylinder, the 28 B.C. tomb of the first Roman emperor, was once clad with marble and planted with elegant rings of cypress trees. Mussolini had designs on making the mausoleum his own family tomb, so he built the surrounding iceberglike travertine buildings to give the area an appropriately harsh Fascist aesthetic. In fact, the Duce had plans to enshrine all the ruins of Rome with such austere honorific architecture—had he remained in power longer, similarly stark facades would appear all over the *centro* today. ⏲ *15 min. Piazza Augusto Imperatore. Ruins open by appointment only.* ☎ *06-67103819. Fax 06-6790795.*

⑥ Largo della Fontanella Borghese. Home to the Mercato delle Stampe antique books market. *See p 86.*

⑦ ★ Streets from Piazza Borghese to Piazza del Parlamento. These dark and narrow alleys seem to breathe ancient intrigue. Indeed, Vicolo del Divino Amore is where the short-tempered painter Caravaggio threw rocks at his landlord's window after a rent dispute. Nearby, Palazzo Firenze is home to the Società Dante Alighieri, the city's most venerable school of Italian for foreigners. *www.dante alighieri-roma.it.*

⑧ ★ Piazza San Lorenzo in Lucina. This cafe-equipped refuge for weary shoppers is home of the eponymous church, where the very grill on which St. Lawrence was barbecued is kept in a side chapel. ⏲ *15 min. Church open daily 9am–noon, 5–7:30pm.*

⑨ Caffè Teichner. Coffee, beer, and light sandwiches are served. Caffè Ciampini, adjacent, is its

virtual twin. *Piazza San Lorenzo in Lucina 17.* ☎ *06-6790612. $–$$.*

🔟 **Via Condotti.** Aided by its deputies, Via Borgognona, Via Bocca di Leone, Via Mario de' Fiori, and Via Belsiana, high-end retail artery Via Condotti spearheads an effort to bring financial ruin on all who dare to carry a credit card near the Spanish Steps.

⓫ **★★★ Piazza di Spagna.** It's de rigueur on any tourist's itinerary, but prepare to contend with perpetual mobs of gelato-wielding tourists and Casanovas trawling the square for naive foreign females. Luckily, neither taints the overall beauty of the glamorously upsweeping Spanish Steps (which were actually designed and funded by the French). At the base of the 18th-century stairs, the sunken *Barcaccia* ("bad boat") fountain is by Pietro Bernini (Gian Lorenzo's father) and fed by the ancient Aqua Virgo. It's reputed to

The Margutta Art Fair, on Via Margutta.

have the sweetest water in Rome. At no. 26 on the piazza is the Keats-Shelley House where Keats died of tuberculosis at the age of 25. Crowning the top of the stairs is the graceful Trinità dei Monti Church. ⏱ *20 min. Piazza di Spagna. Best in early morning or late evening.*

⓬ **★★ Via Margutta.** This impossibly gorgeous lane, nestled between the Pincio and Via del Babuino and lined with artists' ateliers, has sparked many a visitor's fantasy about dropping everything and moving to Rome.

The Trinità dei Monti sits atop the Spanish Steps.

Monti

1 Piazza Madonna dei Monti
2 La Bottega del Caffè
3 Santa Maria dei Monti
4 Mercato Rionale
5 Ancient Wall along Via Tor de' Conti

6 Totti Mural
7 Via degli Zingari and Via Leonina
8 Streets between Via Urban and Via Panisperna
9 Urbana 47

What was once the red-light district of ancient Rome and the poorest part of the city in the Renaissance, Monti is now one of the hippest, most authentic, and least-touristed quarters of Rome's historic core. Century-old butcher shops are adjacent to progressive boutiques and salons, and ethnic eating and classic *enoteche* (wine cellars) abound. START: **Take Metro Line B to Cavour, and then walk.**

1 ★★ **Piazza Madonna dei Monti.** Start your walking tour at Monti's hub of social life and foot and motor traffic. The 16th century fountain here is rather unassuming for Rome, which indicates the level of poverty in this area at the time of its construction.

2 ★★ **La Bottega del Caffè.** When visiting Piazza Madonna dei Monti, do as the locals do and stop for a cappuccino—or a beer, depending on the time of day—at

this vibrant hive of local color. *Piazza Madonna dei Monti 5. $–$$.*

3 **Santa Maria dei Monti.** Across Via dei Serpenti is the piazza's namesake, a church dedicated to Mary and designed in 1580 by Giacomo della Porta, who also designed the more famous Gesù, just west of Piazza Venezia. *Via Madonna dei Monti 14.*

4 ★ **Mercato Rionale.** Monti is one of few remaining *rioni* in the

Piazza Madonna dei Monti.

historic center with its own *mercato*, which indicates the strength of tradition in this community. Some residents have been buying their artichokes and *fior di latte mozzarella* here for centuries.

5 ★★ **Ancient Wall along Via Tor de' Conti.** The massive grey tufa wall running along the south side of the street was erected in 2 B.C. as a firewall and visual barrier between the Suburra (Monti's old moniker) and the glorious Imperial Forums, the ruins of which are visible through breaks in the wall. The Suburra was the ancient city's red-light district and general bad neighborhood—if you've seen HBO's *Rome,* you may have some sense of how rough it was. Unfortunately, the firewall proved ineffectual during the infamous conflagration of A.D. 64, which started in the Suburra and raged for 7 days, destroying two-thirds of the city.

6 ★ **Totti Mural.** You won't find it marked on most maps, but tiny Via del Pozzo dead-ends with a vivid, red-and-yellow mural of homegrown soccer hero Francesco Totti (the captain of A.S. Roma and member of the Italian national team). The iconic image, which depicts Totti kissing his finger and raising it to the sky, was painted on the occasion of *La Roma*'s championship title in 2001.

7 ★ **Via degli Zingari and Via Leonina.** Stroll these narrow streets and browse the cutting-edge boutiques that have cropped up in the neighborhood in recent years and that account for much of its renaissance. Image-conscious women can stop in for a 15€ *piega* (blow-out) at cool Contesta Rock Hair (Via degli Zingari 9).

8 ★ **Streets between Via Urbana and Via Panisperna.** These stepped backstreets—from Via Ciancaleoni to Via Capocci—will make you forget you're in a world capital. Cats sleep on the sidewalk, and women dry their laundry on lines outside their cramped *palazzi*. It's what Trastevere used to look like before the rents went up.

9 **Urbana 47.** Wind up your tour at this modern bohemian cafe, which serves light fare at all hours. *Via Urbana 47.* ☎ *06-47884006. $$.*

The Totti mural on Via del Pozzo.

Jewish Ghetto & Tiber Island

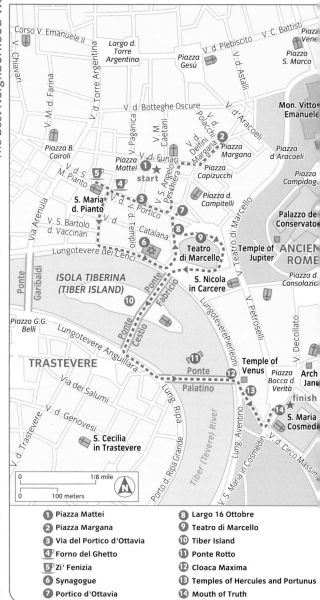

1. Piazza Mattei
2. Piazza Margana
3. Via del Portico d'Ottavia
4. Forno del Ghetto
5. Zi' Fenizia
6. Synagogue
7. Portico d'Ottavia
8. Largo 16 Ottobre
9. Teatro di Marcello
10. Tiber Island
11. Ponte Rotto
12. Cloaca Maxima
13. Temples of Hercules and Portunus
14. Mouth of Truth

Packed with monuments from every era of Roman history, the Jewish Ghetto has left its dark days behind and become a vibrant, rewarding place to explore. Tiber Island and the riverbank here offer rustic charm and some of the city's most interesting, unsung sights. START: **Take bus 30, 40, 62, 64, 70, 87, 116, 492, 571, or 628, or tram 8 to Largo Argentina.**

1 ★★ Piazza Mattei. One of Rome's most prized possessions, the Fontana delle Tartarughe (Tortoise Fountain) lies tucked away in this gem of a square, where you'll often find film crews shooting and art students sketching its picturesquely patinated centerpiece.

2 ★ Piazza Margana. This textbook example of a charming Italian square is complete with geraniums spilling out of window boxes, a pretty alfresco cafe/restaurant—and, if you look carefully down tiny Via di Tor Margana, a gun-barrel view of Trajan's Column, .5km (⅓ mile) away.

3 ★ Via del Portico d'Ottavia. Formerly the eastern boundary of the Jewish Ghetto, this bumpy, busy street is now the principal thoroughfare of the modern neighborhood, with shop signs in Hebrew alluding to the community's heritage.

4 ★ Forno del Ghetto. It's hard to resist the sweet smells of almonds, cinnamon, and ricotta emanating from this tiny Ghetto bakery, run by three gruff matrons. Cookies and candied cakes are sold by the kilo and are best eaten fresh out of the oven. *Via del Portico d'Ottavia 1.* ☎ *06-6878637. $.*

5 ★ Zi' Fenizia. Delicious—and kosher—pizza by the slice is served here, and there are a few stools to sit on while you scarf it down. *Via Santa Maria del Pianto 64.* ☎ *06-6896976. $.*

6 ★★ Synagogue. Rome's gorgeous, palm-treed Sinagoga is a particularly triumphant edifice in this part of town. It was built in the 1890s over land that was once the most squalid part of the Ghetto,

A block of colorful houses in the Jewish Ghetto.

The ceiling of the neo-Babylonian Synagogue of Rome is decorated with ornate metalwork and frescoed palm trees.

shortly after the decree that ended the Jewish segregation. Inside the temple is the Museo d'Arte Ebraica, with vivid exhibits documenting the persecution of the Jews in Rome from 1555—when the papal bull, *Cum nimis absurdum,* established the Ghetto laws—through the Nazi occupation of the 1940s. ⏱ *30 min. Lungotevere Cenci 15.* ☎ *06-68400661. 6€. Sun–Thurs 9am–4:30pm (until 7pm May–Aug), Fri 9am–1:30pm.*

7 ★ **Portico d'Ottavia.** Poking up from the ancient level at the end of Via del Portico d'Ottavia are the impressive remains of a propylaeum (gate to a temple precinct), built by Augustus, and named for his sister, in 23 B.C. Today, the portico is the monumental entry to the modest medieval Church of Sant'Angelo in Pescheria, where Jews were forced to attend Catholic Mass during the Ghetto period. The pavement outside was for centuries the site of Rome's fish market *(pescheria),* hence the name of the church. ⏱ *15 min. Free admission. Excavations daily 9am–5pm.*

8 ★ **Largo 16 Ottobre.** In front of the Portico d'Ottavia ruins, a plaque on the wall commemorates the place where, on the night of October 16, 1943, Roman Jews were rounded up by Nazi troops and deported to the concentration camps of Auschwitz and Birkenau. Of the 3,091 men, women, and children deported, only 15 survived.

9 ★★ **Teatro di Marcello (Theater of Marcellus).** With a 15,000-spectator capacity, this 13-B.C. theater was the main ancient Roman venue for plays, concerts, and the occasional public execution. In the 1300s, the Savelli family built a fortress on top of the ponderous ruins, which they then converted into a palace during the Renaissance. Above the ancient travertine arches, the apartments are still inhabited by modern princes and *contessas.* ⏱ *15 min. Free admission. Excavations daily 9am–5pm.*

10 ★★ **Tiber Island.** In 391 B.C., a snake slithered onto the shores of Tiber Island; at the same time, a decade-long plague in Rome ended. Ever since, the river island has been a sanctuary of medicine, with the Fatebenefratelli Hospital today occupying the majority of the real estate here. The ancient Romans, in a moment of fancy, sculpted the island to look like a ship; part of the "hull" (a fragment of carved travertine) can still be seen on the lower esplanade, a favorite sunning spot of Romans on their lunch breaks. Stairs to the lower esplanade are located west of the main entrance to the hospital. 🕐 *30 min.*

⓫ ★ **Ponte Rotto.** Stranded in the middle of the river below Tiber Island is the single arch of the 142 B.C. Ponte Rotto, or "broken bridge," which fell and was rebuilt so many times that the city finally abandoned it when it collapsed in 1598. From the neighboring modern bridge, Ponte Palatino, wheel ruts can still be seen on the Ponte Rotto's roadway. *No access.*

⓬ **Cloaca Maxima.** A gaping arch in the riverbank walls, under the eastern end of the Ponte Palatino, is the mouth of the 6th-century-B.C. "great sewer," constructed to drain the moisture from the swampy valley of the Roman Forum. According to some archaeologists, the underground waterway is still navigable, with secret access hatches in unlikely parts of the city. *Interior open by appointment only.* ☎ 06-67103819.

⓭ ★ **Temples of Hercules and Portunus.** In a beautiful setting, among oleanders and fountains on a grassy rise near the riverbank, these two Republican-era temples survive because of their reconsecration as churches. For centuries, the round temple (of Hercules) was known as the Temple of Vesta because the only other known round temple was that of Vesta in the Roman Forum. The rectangular temple was dedicated to Portunus, god of port activity; in antiquity, the most important cargo coming to Rome, like columns for the Forum or lions for the Colosseum, was unloaded from river barges here. *No access.*

⓮ ★ **Mouth of Truth.** Propped up at the end of the portico of the Church of Santa Maria in Cosmedin (which has a fantastic Romanesque bell tower and unusual Greek Orthodox interior) is an ancient sewer cover known as the Bocca della Verità (Mouth of Truth), which is supposed to bite off the hands of liars. All day, tourists line up to take pictures of themselves with their hands in the mouth slot—cheesy, but a Roman rite of passage. 🕐 *15 min. Queue shortest before 1pm. Piazza della Bocca della Verità.* ☎ *06-6781419. Free admission. Daily 9am–5pm.*

The bridge to Tiber Island.

Pigneto

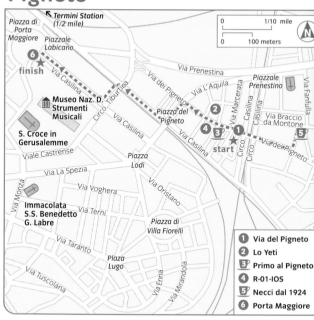

Termini Station (1/2 mile)

Piazza di Porta Maggiore

Piazzale Labicano

Via Prenestina

Piazzale Prenestino

Via Prenestina

6 **finish** Via Casilina

Via dei Pigneto

Via L'Aquila

Via Marcerata

Casilina

Via Braccio da Montone

Museo Naz. D. Strumenti Musicali

Circo. Tiburtina

Via Casilina

Piazza del Pigneto

Via Fanfulla

2

4 **3** **1**

Via Casilina

start

S. Croce in Gerusalemme

Viale Castrense

Circo. Cas...

Via dei Pigneto

5

Via La Spezia

Piazza Lodi

Via Monza

Via Voghera

Via Oristano

Immacolata S.S. Benedetto G. Labre

Via Terni

Piazza di Villa Fiorelli

Via Taranto

Via Enna

Via Mirandola

Plaza Lugo

Via Tuscolana

0 ——— 1/10 mile
0 ——— 100 meters

1	Via del Pigneto
2	Lo Yeti
3	Primo al Pigneto
4	R-01-IOS
5	Necci dal 1924
6	Porta Maggiore

I**f you want to check out what's going on in modern Rome far from the tourist hordes,** take a short bus ride east of Termini to Pigneto, which since 2006 has been the "it" neighborhood for the arbiters of Rome's contemporary culture. Via del Pigneto is the pedestrian-only main strip of this trendily gritty quarter, where Pasolini filmed *Accattone* and Rossellini filmed *Roma Città Aperta.* Nowadays, stylish bars and edgy jewelry shops sit adjacent to the old mom-and-pop hardware stores that sell dust brooms to local housewives. Don't think of this as a tour of "sights"—it's more about being with multiple generations of real Romans doing their thing, far from the chaos of the Spanish Steps and Vatican. START: **Take bus 81 or 105 or tram 5, 14, or 19. Day to avoid: Monday, when almost everything's closed.**

1 ★★ **Via del Pigneto.** The .8km-long (½-mile) main drag of Pigneto, closed to automobile traffic, is where you'll find most of the area's bars, shops, and restaurants. For the best people-watching, come on a late Sunday afternoon, when you can join tons of locals out for a *passeggiata* (stroll) and an *aperitivo.*

2 ★ **Lo Yeti.** This low-key cafe/bookshop is a good place to sample the Pigneto vibe and find out what's on, events-wise. They host or sponsor a lot of cultural happenings, from Roman folk-music concerts to avant-garde film screenings. There's also an Internet point. *Via Perugia 4.* ☎ *06-7025633. Closed Mon.*

3 ★★ Primo al Pigneto. The premier "cool new restaurant" of Pigneto (opened in 2006) serves beautifully presented modern Italian cuisine. Chef/owner Marco Gallotta's creations have received tons of positive press among local food critics. Come for a full meal or just a snack and drink. *Via del Pigneto 46.* ☎ 06-7013827. *Closed Mon. $$–$$$.*

4 ★ R-01-IOS. Flagship store of edgy jewelry maker Losselliani, whose collections are sold in the trendiest boutiques from Tokyo to L.A. The multichain necklaces and stacking rings (priced from 200€) ooze style. *Via del Pigneto 36.* ☎ 06-70613527. *Open 6pm–midnight. Closed Sun–Mon.*

5 ★★ Necci dal 1924. This retro-chic bar/restaurant—a favorite of film types since the '50s—is a great casual hangout any time of day. Grab a table inside and admire the movie memorabilia, or sit outside, shaded by trees in the front garden, and watch local life roll by on this secluded side street. Feel free to bring a book or laptop to go along with your Campari and soda. *Via Fanfulla da Lodi 68.* ☎ 06-97601552. *$–$$.*

6 ★★ Porta Maggiore. Not part of Pigneto proper, but within reasonable walking distance, this travertine gateway was first built by emperor Claudius in A.D. 52 as a monument to mark the point of entry into the city of the Aqua Claudia and Aqua Anio Novus aqueducts. Look at the top of the monument and you'll see the hollow channels where the water flowed. (The Latin inscription congratulates Claudius, as well as later emperors Vespasian and Titus, for their contributions to city waterworks.) Two centuries later, the freestanding gateway was incorporated into Rome's Aurelian Walls. Immediately southeast of Porta Maggiore is the one-of-a-kind **Tomb of Eurysaces**—look for the white structure with uniform round holes along the sides. Eurysaces was a freedman and baker in 1st-century-B.C. Rome, and the cylinders have been interpreted as models of grain measures or vessels for mixing dough. Some friezes with scenes of the baking life are preserved at the top of the tomb. *Tram 3 or 19.*

The popular Necci dal 1924 is a great stop for a drink or a bite.

Testaccio

1 Pyramid of Gaius Cestius
2 Porta San Paolo
3 Protestant Cemetery
4 Il Seme e la Foglia
5 Monte Testaccio
6 Via di Monte Testaccio
7 Mattatoio
8 Mercato di Testaccio
9 Sora Rosa

Testaccio, whose most salient physical features are a defunct slaughterhouse, an ancient rubbish heap, and a slew of nightclubs, has long been a working-class bastion of real Romans and average architecture. Although it's become one of Rome's shabby-chic "in" neighborhoods, Testaccio's salt-of-the-earth flavor remains. START: **Take Metro Line B, bus 23, 30, 170, 271, or 280, or tram 3 to Piramide/Piazzale Ostiense.**

❶ ★ Pyramid of Gaius Cestius.
Egyptomania was all the rage in 1st-century-B.C. Rome, and though none would mistake this rather incongruous spike of white marble for the pyramids of Giza, the Roman magistrate who had it built as his tomb probably intended to have it taken just as seriously. *Open by appointment only.* ☎ *06-67103819. Fax 06-6790795.*

❷ ★ Porta San Paolo.
One of the best-preserved gateways from the 3rd-century-A.D. Aurelian Walls, this is home to the small Museo di Via Ostiense, with interesting artifacts relating to Roman roads. ⏱ *20 min. Piazzale Ostiense/Via R. Persichetti 3.* ☎ *06-5743193. Free admission. Opening hours vary.*

The Pyramid of Gaius Cestius.

❸ ★ Protestant Cemetery.
Just beyond a ruined stretch of the Aurelian Walls, the charming *Cimitero Acattolico* complies with the ancient mandate that all burials be outside the city limits. Its peaceful, totally unexpected grounds are home to the graves of Percy Bysshe Shelley, who drowned off the Italian Riviera in 1822 before his 30th birthday; John Keats; and Antonio Gramsci, founder of the Italian Communist Party, among others. *Via Caio Cestio 6.* ☎ *06-5741900. Donation expected. Tues–Sun 9am–4:30pm.*

❹ ★ Il Seme e la Foglia.
Opposite Monte Testaccio, this cafe offers monstrous salads, beers on tap, and great local flavor. *Via Galvani 18.* ☎ *06-5743008. $–$$.*

❺ ★★ Monte Testaccio.
One of the ancient Romans' most remarkable creations, the "Monte dei Cocci" (Hill of Shards) is an artificial mountain, 30m high (100 ft.), made entirely of broken amphorae (slender vessels used to transport oil and wine) that were discarded here over centuries of importation. There's a good view of the red clay shards through the gates at the corner of Via Galvani and Via Zabaglia, and through the back walls of many of the clubs and bars built against the hill. *Via Zabaglia 24. Open by appointment only.* ☎ *06-67103819. Fax 06-6790795.*

Fish for sale in the Mercato di Testaccio.

6 ★ **Via di Monte Testaccio.** Only in Rome: By night, this is disco central; by day, livestock bleat happily in their pens on the hillside, directly above the shuttered nightclubs where techno beats blared hours earlier.

7 ★ **Il Mattatoio.** Rome's decommissioned abattoir—still recognizable by the statue of a naked hero slaughtering a hapless ox atop its neoclassical facade—is now an exhibition space for a variety of contemporary cultural endeavors, under the aegis of MACRO (Museo d'Arte Contemporaneo di Roma). *Piazza O. Giustiniani. No phone. Hours and prices depend on exhibition.*

8 ★★ **Mercato di Testaccio.** Mingle with local matrons decked out in their finest housedresses and bedroom slippers at the lively covered market at Piazza Testaccio. Then take a walk on Via di Monte Testaccio (bullet **6** in this tour), the circular road that skirts the base of the "mountain made of pottery." *Mon–Sat 7am–1pm.*

9 ★ **Sora Rosa.** Don't leave Testaccio without having smiling Sandro make you a sandwich at his delightful throwback of a snack bar. Join little old men sipping wine (poured from a spigot in the marble wall) and eating generously stuffed panini that won't cost you more than 2€. *Via Galileo Ferraris 7. Closed Sun. $.* ●

Shopping Best Bets

Best **Multi-Label Boutique**
★★ Gente, *Via del Babuino 81* (p 82)

Best **Stylish & Affordable Shoes**
★★★ Martina Novelli, *Piazza Risorgimento 38 (p 88)*; and ★★ Posto Italiano, *Via Giubbonari 37A (p 88)*

Best **Wine Shop**
★★★ Trimani, *Via Goito 20 (p 85)*

Best **Street for Contemporary Fashion**
Via Giubbonari (off Campo de' Fiori)

Best **Accessories at Good Prices**
★ COIN, *Via Cola di Rienzo 173 (p 84)*

Best **Museum Store**
★★ Capitoline Museums, *Piazza del Campidoglio (p 31)*

Best **Teen Threads**
★ Brandy Melville, *Via Cola di Rienzo 136*, and ★ Energie, *Via del Corso 408–409 (p 81)*

Best **Toys and Children's Books**
★★ Città del Sole, *Via della Scrofa 65 (p 88)*

Best **Papal Vestments**
★★ Ghezzi, *Via de' Cestari 32/33 (p 87)*

Best **Gourmet Foods**
★★★ Franchi, *Via Cola di Rienzo 204 (p 85)*; and ★★★ Volpetti, *Via Marmorata 47 (p 86)*

Best **Local Market**
★★★ Piazza Testaccio (p 86)

Best **Gifts**
★★★ Modigliani, *Via Condotti 24 (p 85)*

The bold facade of the COIN department store.

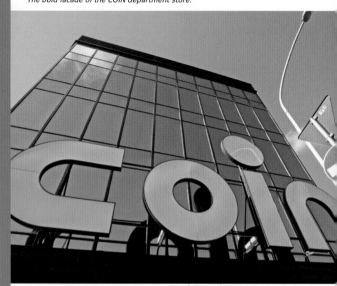

Previous page: A display window at Prada.

Centro Storico Shopping

Ai Monasteri 2	Ethic 5	People 16
Al Sogno 3	Feltrinelli 8	Pinko 12
Campo de' Fiori 17	Ghezzi 7	Posto Italiano 15
Città del Sole 4	L.E.I. 13	Prototype 14
Davide Cenci 1	Limoni 10	Sole 19
Degli Effetti 6	Loco 20	Spazio Sette 11
Ditta G. Poggi 9	Nuyorica 18	

Rome Shopping

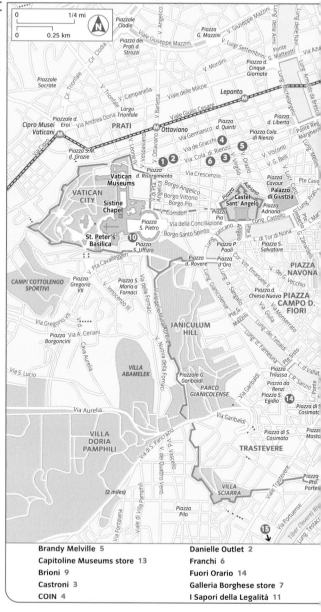

	1/4 mi
0	0.25 km

Piazzale Clodio

Piazza G. Mazzini

Piazza d. Cinque Giornate

Piazzale Socrate

Piazza dei Prati d. Strozzi

Piazzale d. Eroi

Cipro Musei Vaticani

PRATI

Ottaviano

Lepanto

Piazza d. Quiriti

Piazza Cola di Rienzo

Piazza d. Liberta

VATICAN CITY

Vatican Museums

Sistine Chapel

St. Peter's Basilica

Piazza S. Pietro

Piazza Cavour

Palazzo di Giustizia

Castel Sant' Angelo

Piazza S. Salvatore

PIAZZA NAVONA

CAMPI COTTOLENGO SPORTIVI

JANICULUM HILL

PIAZZA CAMPO D. FIORI

VILLA ABAMELEK

PARCO GIANICOLENSE

TRASTEVERE

VILLA DORIA PAMPHILI

VILLA SCIARRA

Brandy Melville 5	Danielle Outlet 2
Capitoline Museums store 13	Franchi 6
Brioni 9	Fuori Orario 14
Castroni 3	Galleria Borghese store 7
COIN 4	I Sapori della Legalità 11

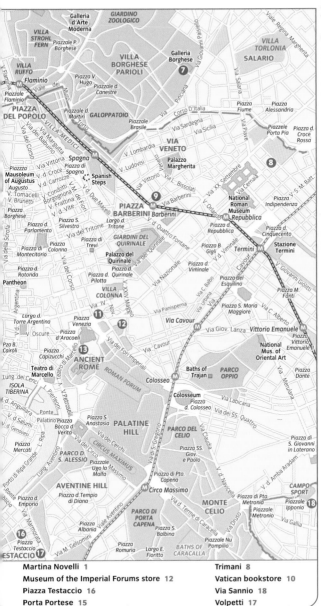

Martina Novelli 1	**Trimani** 8
Museum of the Imperial Forums store 12	**Vatican bookstore** 10
Piazza Testaccio 16	**Via Sannio** 18
Porta Portese 15	**Volpetti** 17

Spanish Steps Shopping

Rome Shopping **A to Z**

Apparel & Accessories

★ **Armani Jeans** SPANISH STEPS
Armani for the rest of us: fun, well-cut clothes in cotton and denim for men and women at humane prices. *Via Tomacelli 137 (at Largo degli Schiavoni).* ☎ 06-3222249. www. armani.com. AE, MC, V. Metro: Spagna. Bus: 492 or 628. Map p 80.

★ **Brandy Melville** VATICAN
Sort of like Abercrombie meets Juicy Couture meets J. Crew, this Italian label with a cultlike following is where Rome's privileged teens go for Lindsay Lohan-esque staples like striped T-shirts, tanks, leggings, and underwear. A must for the young fashionista on your shopping list. *Via Cola di Rienzo 136 (at Via Orazio).* ☎ 06-3211622. AE, MC, V. Metro: Ottaviano. Bus: 70, 81. Map p 78.

★★ **Brioni** PIAZZA BARBERINI
You're in excellent (if expensive) hands at this custom men's clothier—the same sartorial masters who have tailored the suits of every dashing 007 from Connery to Brosnan. *Via Barberini 79–81 (at Piazza Barberini).* ☎ 06-485855. AE, MC, V. Metro: Barberini. Map p 78.

A couple shopping on Via Condotti.

★★ **Davide Cenci** PANTHEON
At this Roman emporium of classic men's and women's wear, Ralph Lauren sweaters, Fay coats, Pucci dresses, and Cenci's own label shirts, country clubbers feel right at home. *Via Campo Marzio 1–7 (at Via*

VAT Refund

If you're a non-EU citizen and spend 151€ or more at any one retailer, you're entitled to the VAT refund, which knocks 11% to 13% off your bill. (This is handy if you, like me, are always trying to find ways to rationalize extravagant purchases.) In order to get your refund, you must 1) obtain a completed tax-free form from the store, and 2) present your unused purchases for inspection at the airport (in Rome or your last European port). The inspector will stamp your form, which then enables you to pick up a **cash refund** on the spot at the airport, or to file for a **credit card adjustment,** which can take up to 90 days to process.

Shoppers display their Energie shopping bag.

Uffici del Vicario). ☎ 06-6990681. AE, MC, V. Bus: 62, 85, 95, 175, or 492. Map p 77.

★ **Energie** PIAZZA DEL POPOLO With labels like Miss Sixty and Killah, the brash and bright fashions here are meant for teens, but you'll find many a Roman mom in here buying something for herself along with jeans for her 15-year-old son. *Via del Corso 408–409 (at Via del Vantaggio).* ☎ 06-6871258. AE, MC, V. Metro: Flaminio. Map p 80.

★ **Ethic** PANTHEON A favorite of 20- and 30-something Roman women, with reasonably priced boho-chic pieces in saturated colors and adherent cuts. *Via del Pantheon*

46–47 (at Piazza della Maddalena). ☎ 06-68803167. (Branch at Piazza Cairoli 11–12, at Via Giubbonari. ☎ 06-68301063.) AE, MC, V. Bus: 30, 40, 62, 64, 70, 85, 87, 95, 116, 175, or 492. Map p 77.

★ **Fuori Orario** TRASTEVERE This tiny corner shop has a kaleidoscopic array of leather jackets, plus inexpensive, trendy apparel by French designers. Discounts for cash payment are often available. *Via del Moro 29 (at Via della Pelliccia).* ☎ 06-5817181. MC, V. Bus: 23, 271, or 280. Map p 78.

★★ **Gente** SPANISH STEPS A microcosm of the Via Condotti boutiques, with more affordable denim and accessories. *Via del Babuino 81 (at Piazza di Spagna).* ☎ 06-3207671. AE, MC, V. Metro: Spagna. (Branch at Via Cola di Rienzo 277, Vatican area.) Map p 80.

★★ **L.E.I.** CAMPO DE' FIORI Should one of Rome's remaining princes invite you to the ball, come here first for a feast of frocks, in all shapes and all price ranges. *Via Giubbonari 103 (at Via dei Chiavari).* ☎ 06-6875432. AE, MC, V. Bus: 30, 40, 62, 64, 70, 87, or 492. (Branch at Via Nazionale 88.) Map p 77.

Ethic, a popular stop for fashionable, yet budget-conscious women.

Sale Season

If you come to Rome in late January and late July, you might not find the best weather, but if you're a shopper, your timing is perfect. All stores in Italy have two annual liquidation periods *(saldi)*, during which there are serious deals to be had. Discounts start at 30% (though most are 50%) and can go as deep as 75% off regular retail. The best part is that these sale items are not chartreuse raincoats or other fashion faux pas; we're talking regular, desirable merchandise, yours for the taking at two magical times per year. Without waiting in long lines, traveling to suburban outlets, or pawing through piles of cast-offs, I've made off with Dolce & Gabbana pumps, Pucci sandals, and Max Mara jackets for proverbial pennies.

★ **Murphy & Nye** PIAZZA DEL POPOLO   Roman men love to dress as if they're on a back-up crew for a major regatta. Join 'em with threads from this trendy, nautical-inspired sportswear boutique. *Via del Corso 26–27 (near Piazza del Popolo).* ☎ 06-36004461. AE, MC, V. Metro: Flaminio. Map p 80.

★★ **Nuyorica** CAMPO DE' FIORI With carefully selected clothes, bags, and shoes by such A-list designers as Marni and Balenciaga, this startlingly hip boutique shows just how far the Campo de' Fiori area has come from its humble roots. *Piazza Pollarola 36–37 (at Via del Biscione).* ☎ 06-68891243. www.nuyorica.it. AE, MC, V. Bus: 30, 40, 62, 64, 70, 87, or 492. Map p 77.

★★ **People** CAMPO DE' FIORI   By far the best vintage clothing store in town. For those who can't deal with that pre-owned smell, the boutique also sells new clothing with retro styling—think dresses that look like 1960s Pucci. *Piazza Teatro di Pompeo 4A (at Via dei Chiavari).* ☎ 06-6874040. AE, MC, V. Bus: 30, 40, 62, 64, 70, 87, 116, or 492. Map p 77.

★★ **Pinko** CAMPO DE' FIORI Embellished knits, deconstructed denim, and great pants in mineral tones are the hallmark of this Northern Italian women's label. *Via Giubbonari 76–77 (at Campo de' Fiori).* ☎ 06-68309446. www.pinko.it. AE, DC, MC, V. Bus: 30, 40, 62, 64, 70, 87, or 492. Map p 77.

★ **Prototype** CAMPO DE' FIORI The owners of this unisex boutique scour the land to bring hip and colorful casual wear and sneakers to Roman 20- and 30-somethings. *Via Giubbonari 50 (at Campo de' Fiori).* ☎ 06-68300330. AE, MC, V. Bus: 30, 40, 62, 64, 70, 87, or 492. Tram: 8. Map p 77.

★ **Sole** CAMPO DE' FIORI   Glam women's accessories and clothing with Italian attitude—think sassy, bejeweled handbags and snug-fitting fur-trimmed trenches—make for fabulous I-picked-this-up-in-Rome purchases. *Via dei Baullari 21 (at Piazza della Cancelleria).* ☎ 06-68806987. AE, MC, V. Bus: 30, 40, 62, 64, 70, 87, 116, or 492. Map p 77.

★★ **TAD** SPANISH STEPS   Everything in this lifestyle "concept" boutique, which looks like a lush, glossy magazine spread, is for sale, from the Lucite pumps to the bamboo trees. The in-store cafe and hair salon give you even more ways to spend your euros. *Via del Babuino 155A (at Via dei Greci).* ☎ 06-32695122. www.taditaly.com. *AE, MC, V. Metro: Spagna. Map p 80.*

Books

★★ Anglo-American Book Co.
SPANISH STEPS   English-language titles of all kinds are sold here, but the selection is particularly strong on art and architecture. *Via della Vite 102 (at Via Mario de' Fiori).* ☎ 06-6795222. *AE, MC, V. Metro: Spagna. Map p 80.*

★ Feltrinelli Libri e Musica
PANTHEON   With bar-code-scanning CD listening stations and a great travel section, Rome has its answer to Borders in this renovated branch of a national book chain. Quite novel for Italy, there's also an in-store cafe. *Largo di Torre Argentina 5A–6 (at Corso Vittorio Emanuele II).* ☎ 06-68803248. *AE, MC, V. Bus: 30, 40, 62, 64, 70, 87, or 492. Map p 77.*

★ Libreria Godel
TREVI FOUNTAIN New and used books for tourists and scholars, plus cool retro Vespa clocks and calendars with 1950s Italian advertising motifs. *Via Poli 46 (at Piazza Poli).* ☎ 06-6798716. *AE, MC, V. Bus: 62, 63, 85, 95, 175, 492. Map p 80.*

Department Stores

★ COIN
VATICAN   It's underwhelming if you're used to the U.S. or U.K. department store standard, but COIN does have some great finds in its accessories section, where the latest looks in handbags and belts are very budget-friendly. Look for deals on housewares and makeup, too. *Via Cola di Rienzo 173 (at Via Paolo Emilio).* ☎ 06-700020. *AE, MC, V. Metro: Ottaviano. Map p 78.*

★ La Rinascente
SPANISH STEPS Similar to COIN but larger and more central, La Rinascente is a good bet when you need to buy a last-minute leather wallet or silk scarf for someone back home. No need to go upstairs: The clothing floors are Frumpsville. *Largo Chigi 20 (at Via del Corso).* ☎ 06-6797691. *AE, MC, V. Bus: 62, 63, 85, 95, 175, or 492. Map p 80.*

Design & Home Furnishings

★★ C.U.C.I.N.A.
SPANISH STEPS At this shrine to stainless-steel cookware and kitchen gadgets, you can pick up authentic Bialetti stove-top coffeemakers, mini-parmigiano graters, and all gauges of ravioli-cutters. *Via Mario de' Fiori 65 (at Via delle Carrozze).* ☎ 06-6791275.

The colorful entranceway to the TAD lifestyle "concept" boutique.

High Fashion Boutiques

All roads lead to Rome; the roads around the Spanish Steps lead to credit card debt. Leading the luxury retail pack is Via Condotti, which boasts the boutiques of **Alberta Ferretti, Armani, Dior, Dolce & Gabbana, Ferragamo, Gucci, Hermès, La Perla, Louis Vuitton, Max Mara, Prada, Valentino, YSL,** and the massive **Fendi** flagship, anchoring the western end of the street. Piazza di Spagna weighs in with **Roberto Cavalli, D&G, Escada, Frette, Missoni,** and **Sergio Rossi**; while Via Babuino has **Chanel, Etro, Giuseppe Zanotti,** and **Prada Sport.** Nearby Via Borgognona is graced by the doors of **Givenchy, Loro Piana, Tod's,** and **Versace**; and Via Belsiana features **Moschino.**

www.cucinastore.com. *AE, MC, V. Metro: Spagna. Map p 80.*

★★★ **Modigliani** SPANISH STEPS From Murano wineglasses to hand-painted Tuscan platters, the fine (but not fussy) merchandise at this four-story tabletop-goods store makes great gifts that can be shipped anywhere in the world. *Via Condotti 24 (at Via Bocca di Leone).* ☎ 06-6785653. www.modigliani.it. *AE, MC, V. Metro: Spagna. Map p 80.*

★★ **Spazio Sette** CAMPO DE' FIORI The hottest Italian design, in everything from sofas to picture frames, reigns supreme at this three-floor housewares emporium. *Via dei Barbieri 7 (at Largo Argentina).* ☎ 06-68804261. *AE, MC, V. Bus: 30, 40, 62, 64, 70, 87, or 492. Map p 77.*

Food & Wine
★★ **Castroni** VATICAN This coffee bar extraordinaire has bulk candy, caviar, fine wines, and all manner of oils and vinegars. A godsend for many expats, Castroni also stocks hard-to-get foreign foodstuffs like Bisquick and Vegemite. *Via Cola di Rienzo 196–198 (at Via Terenzio).* ☎ 06-6874383. *AE, MC, V. Metro: Ottaviano. Map p 78.*

★★★ **Franchi** VATICAN One of the top two gourmet delis in town (Volpetti is the other), Franchi has every cheese and cured meat under the sun. At lunch, hot prepared food (including heavenly *supplì*) is available to go. *Via Cola di Rienzo 204 (at Via Terenzio).* ☎ 06-6874651. *AE, MC, V. Metro: Ottaviano. Map p 78.*

★ **I Sapori della Legalità** PIAZZA VENEZIA/ANCIENT ROME "The Flavors of Legality" is a politically charged, little-known shop selling olive oil, tomato sauce, and dry pasta made on lands, in Sicily and southern Italy, that Italian organized-crime fighters have confiscated from the Mafia. Great for the *Godfather* buffs back home! *Via del Foro di Traiano 84 (off Via dei Fori Imperiali).* ☎ 06-69925262. *AE, MC, V. Bus: 40, 60, 85, 87, or 175. Map p 78.*

★★★ **Trimani** TERMINI Founded in 1821 and still run by the same family, this is Rome's best wine shop. The knowledgeable owners can help you navigate the overwhelming selection. *Via Goito 20 (at Via Cernaia).* ☎ 06-4469661. *AE, MC, V. Metro: Castro Pretorio. Bus: 60, 75, or 492. Map p 78.*

Museum Stores

When it comes to only-in-Rome gifts and souvenirs, steer clear of the tchotchke street vendors and head to one of the city's excellent museum bookshops. Some of the best are at the **Capitoline Museums** (p 31), the new **Museum of the Imperial Forums** at Trajan's Markets (p 24), and the **Galleria Borghese** (p 30). The **Vatican bookstore,** on the south side of St. Peter's Square, has a dizzying array of art books, religious tomes, rosaries, and "pope-phernalia."

★★★ **Volpetti** TESTACCIO   Foodies, prepare to swoon—the aromas of cheese and cured meat here beckon like at no other deli in Rome. The enthusiastic staff will let you taste everything, a lovely and sneaky tactic that just gets you to spend more money. An amazing selection of honeys, vinegars, Italian spirits, pâtés, preserves, infused oils, and truffled items. *Via Marmorata 47 (at Via Alessandro Volta).* ☎ *06-5742352. AE, MC, V. Metro: Piramide. Bus: 23, 30, 75, 95, 271, or 280. Tram: 3. Map p 78.*

Markets

★★ **Campo de' Fiori**   This historic produce market is still a Roman institution and well worth a visit, though kitschy souvenir aprons and

all manner of kitchen tools have begun to take over what used to be the city's most authentic fruit-and-veg bazaar. *Mon–Sat 7am–2pm. No credit cards. Bus: 30, 40, 62, 64, 70, 87, or 492. Map p 77.*

★★ **Mercato delle Stampe** PIAZZA DEL POPOLO   Here you'll find wonderfully worn antique books, old engravings, vintage magazines, and their loving dealers. To get the best price, feign some sort of expertise in the print market. *Largo della Fontanella Borghese. No credit cards. Metro: Spagna. Bus: 81. Map p 80.*

★★★ **Piazza Testaccio**   In salt-of-the-earth Testaccio, this covered market is the real deal. Women in housedresses greet everyone by name as they shuffle from butchers'

Blocks of Parmesan cheese.

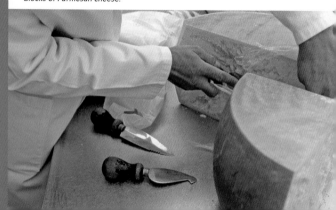

stalls to produce stands, where their inevitable laments over the rising cost of zucchini blossoms are pure theater. *Mon–Sat 7am–1pm. No credit cards. Metro: Piramide. Bus: 23, 75, or 170. Tram: 3.*

★ **Porta Portese** TRASTEVERE Unless you're in the market for a Turkish casino ashtray or a dot-matrix printer, you'll find Rome's biggest flea market more spectacle than practical shopping experience. *Via Portuense (from Piazza Porta Portese to Via Ettore Rolli). Sun only 7am–2pm. No credit cards. Bus: 23, 271, or 280. Tram: 3 or 8. Map p 78.*

★ **Via Sannio** SAN GIOVANNI Good for new and used clothes, leather jackets, and shoes. *Via Sannio. Mon–Sat 10am–2pm. No credit cards. Metro: San Giovanni. Map p 78.*

Perfumeries
★★ **Ai Monasteri** PIAZZA NAVONA In a space that recalls a medieval apothecary, choose from potions, elixirs, candles, and sweets—all made by Italian monks. *Corso Rinascimento 72 (at Piazza Cinque Lune). ☎ 06-68802783. AE, MC, V. Bus: 30, 70, 87, 492, or 628. Map p 77.*

★ **Limoni** PIAZZA VENEZIA/PANTHEON If you forgot to pack your shampoo or toothpaste, this national chain carries basic toiletries that also make for easy souvenirs—people back home always get a kick out of Italian Aqua Fresh. *Corso Vittorio Emanuele 91 (near Via di Torre Argentina). ☎ 06-68210952. AE, MC, V. Bus: 30, 40, 70, 87, 492, 571, or 628. Map p 77.*

Religious Goods
★★ **Ghezzi** PANTHEON Couture cassocks, fab fonts, and marvelous monstrances. Unlike other liturgical outfitters on this street, Ghezzi

A nun admires the flowers on display in the Campo de' Fiori market.

welcomes even laypeople to scope (but not buy) its glorious inventory of all things relating to Catholic ceremony. *Via de' Cestari 32–33 (at Via dell'Arco della Ciambella). ☎ 06-6869744. www.arredi-sacri.it. Bus: 30, 40, 62, 64, 70, 87, 116, or 492. Map p 77.*

Shoes
★ **Danielle Outlet** VATICAN Tight on funds but can't bear to leave Rome without a new pair of shoes? Fear not; this miniscule shop has of-the-moment pairs for under 30€—just don't expect the shoes to last much longer than the trend does. *Piazza Risorgimento 37 (at Via Ottaviano). ☎ 06-39744675. AE, MC, V. Bus: 23, 81, 271, or 492. Tram: 19. Map p 78.*

★★ **Loco** CAMPO DE' FIORI If Dorothy lived in Rome, she might well find her ruby slippers at this wild and wonderful (and pricey) shoe boutique. Classy, unique men's styles available, too. *Via dei Baullari 22 (at Campo de' Fiori). ☎ 06-68808216. AE, MC, V. Bus: 30, 40, 62, 64, 70, 87, 116, 492, or 571. Map p 77.*

"Bambola," one of the amazingly lifelike dolls sold at Al Sogno.

★★★ **Martina Novelli** VATICAN Delightfully opinionated shop girls help women choose the right pair at this hip, mostly affordable shoe store near the Vatican. *Piazza Risorgimento 38 (at Via Ottaviano).* ☎ *06-39737247. AE, MC, V. Bus: 23, 81, 271, or 492. Tram: 19. Map p 78.*

★★ **Posto Italiano** CAMPO DE' FIORI   This friendly "Italian place" stocks well-priced and current shoes and boots for men and women. *Via Giubbonari 37A (off Campo de' Fiori).* ☎ *06-6869373. (Branch: Viale Trastevere 111.* ☎ *06-58334820.) AE, MC, V. Bus: 30, 40, 62, 64, 70, 87, or 492. Map p 77.*

★★ **Vic Matiè/O.X.O.** SPANISH STEPS   Come here for edgy, wearable shoes and boots for men and women that will make your friends back home jealous of your cool, Euro style. Most pairs under 200€. *Via Frattina 96 (at Via Belsiana).* ☎ *06-6790168. (Branch: Via Giubbonari 53.* ☎ *06-64760231.) AE, MC, V. Metro: Spagna. Map p 80.*

Stationers
★ **Campo Marzio Design** PANTHEON   These colorful leatherbound notebooks and pens worthy of Dante himself might just inspire you to keep a journal of your visit to Rome. *Via Campo Marzio 41 (at Piazza San Lorenzo in Lucina).* ☎ *06-68807877. www.campo marzio design.it. AE, MC, V. Bus: 62, 63, 85, 116, or 492. Map p 80.*

★★ **Ditta G. Poggi** PANTHEON Allow plenty of time to peruse the shelves at this 180-year-old art-supplies store. Amid tubes of oil paint and stencils, you might stumble across charming 1950s composition books (at 1950s prices) and the odd Italian BEWARE OF DOG sign. *Via del Gesù 74–75 (at Via Pie' di Marmo).* ☎ *06-6793674. www. poggi1825.it. AE, MC, V. Bus: 30, 40, 62, 64, 70, 87, or 492. Map p 77.*

Toys
★★ **Al Sogno** PIAZZA NAVONA What Santa's workshop must have looked like 50 years ago—this fantastic high-end toyshop amazes young and old alike with its collectible gnomes, life-sized stuffed animals, and themed chess sets. *Piazza Navona 53 (at north end).* ☎ *06-6864198. AE, MC, V. Bus: 30, 70, 87, 492, or 628. Map p 77.*

★★ **Città del Sole** PANTHEON Italy's excellent educational toy and children's books chain invites even adults to spend hours browsing its wonderful merchandise. Teach junior some *italiano* with translated versions of Dr. Seuss and *Where the Wild Things Are. Via della Scrofa 65.* ☎ *06-68803805. AE, MC, V. Bus: 30, 70, 87, 492, or 628. Map p 77.* ●

5 The **Great Outdoors**

Villa Borghese

1. Porta Pinciana
2. Viale del Museo Borghese
3. Piazza di Siena
4. Temple of Diana
5. Laghetto
6. Temple of Aesculapius
7. Caffè delle Arti
8. Piazzale delle Canestre/ Viale delle Magnolie

Previous page: Along the Appian Way.

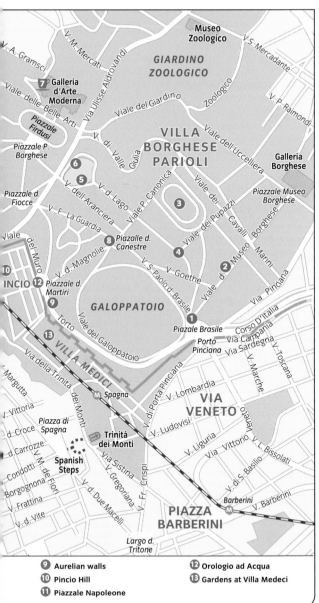

Museo
Zoologico

GIARDINO
ZOOLOGICO

V. A. Gramsci

V. M. Mercati

V. S. Mercadante

Viale delle Belle Arti

Via Ulisse Aldrovandi

Viale del Giardino

Zoologico

V. P. Raimondi

Piazzale
Firdusi

Piazzale P.
Borghese

V. di Valle

Giulia

VILLA
BORGHESE
PARIOLI

Viale dell'Uccelliera

Galleria
Borghese

Piazzale d.
Fiocce

6

5

V. dell'Aranciera

V. d. Lago

Viale P. Canonica

Viale dei

3

Piazzale Museo
Borghese

V. F. La Guardia

8 Piazalle d.
Canestre

Viale dei Pupazzi

Cavalli

Museo Borghese

Marini

Viale
del Muro

V. d. Magnolie

4

V. S. Paolo d. Brasile

V. Goethe

Viale d.

2

Via Pinciana

10
INCIO

12 Piazzale d.
Martiri

9

GALOPPATOIO

1

Corso D'Italia

V. Toscana

Torto

Viale del Galoppatoio

Piazale Brasile

Porto
Pinciana

Via Campania

Via Sardegna

V. Marche

13 VILLA MEDICI

Via della Trinita dei Monti

M Spagna

V. di Porta Pinciana

V. Lombardia

VIA
VENETO

V. Margutta

V. Vittoria

Piazza di
Spagna

d. Croce

d. Carrozze

Trinità
dei Monti

V. Ludovisi

V. Liguria

Via

Vittorio

V. L. Bissolati

Spanish
Steps

Condotti

Borgognona

V. M. de Fiori

Via Sistina

V. Gregoriana

V. Fr. Crispi

V. di S. Basilio

V. Frattina

V. d. Vite

V. d. Due Macelli

Barberini

V. Barberini

PIAZZA
BARBERINI

M

Largo d.
Tritone

Other Roman parks are larger, wilder, and less crowded, but none is as treasured by the city as the gorgeous, glamorous Villa Borghese. Gracing the higher ground directly above the *centro storico,* the Villa Borghese became public property in 1901, when the once-powerful Borghese family ran into financial trouble and sold their estate, complete with its museums, fountains, and faux temples, to the city. The park offers myriad recreation opportunities, with shady lanes, open fields, a lake, a zoo, even a balloon ride; and bikes, *risciò* (rickshaws that you pedal), in-line skates, and rowboats can be rented at several facilities in the park. Bordering some of the city's wealthiest neighborhoods, the Villa Borghese is also the preferred jogging ground—groomed and level—of the Roman rich and famous. **Daily 6am–sunset. Bus: 116 or 490.**

1 Porta Pinciana. Enter the park here, at the top of Via Veneto, just beyond the ancient walls.

Shady, hedge-lined **2 Viale del Museo Borghese** leads to the Galleria Borghese (p 30). When the Borghese family sold their estate to the city, they insisted on a proviso that would preserve the integrity of their magnificent collection of baroque and ancient art in the galleria. On either side of the road are grassy fields, popular with picnickers, sunbathers, and lovers.

Skip the moroseness of the outdated zoo and head west down Viale dei Pupazzi past the elegant

3 Piazza di Siena, where joggers plod (and, in May, horses jump) around a track rimmed with umbrella pines.

At the **4 Temple of Diana** (a 17th-c. faux temple to the ancient goddess of the hunt), turn right, and go north to the man-made **5 Laghetto,** whose northern shore is graced by the picturesque 17th-century **6 Temple of Aesculapius,** the pagan god of medicine. Rent a boat (daily 9am–sunset; 3€ per person for 20 min.) and enjoy a relaxing row around the lake.

The Porta Pinciana is nestled within the ancient walls.

Boating nearby a faux-classical temple in the gardens of the Villa Borghese.

 **Caffè delle Arti** is surrounded by trees and the white marble of the modern art gallery, with alfresco tables perfect for a romantic interlude. There's a lunch buffet with light and savory fare; stop in any time for a coffee, beer, or cocktail. *Via Gramsci 73–75 (at Viale delle Belle Arti). Closed Mon. $$.*

After your snack, retrace your steps past the *laghetto* to  **Piazzale delle Canestre** and **Viale delle Magnolie,** a favorite haunt of strolling Roman families and their cuter-than-thou *bambini.* This pedestrianized avenue is often tricked out with low-lying obstacle courses for skaters and bladers, so be careful of Coke-can slaloms underfoot.

Continue to the bridge that crosses Viale del Muro Torto ("Street of the Crooked Wall") and its namesake, the 3rd-century-A.D.  **Aurelian Walls,** behind which lies  **Pincio Hill,** whose primary attraction is the knockout vista at  **Piazzale Napoleone.** Gaze past the terrace parapets to the ochre rooftops of Rome and the dome of St. Peter's. *See p 43, bullet .*

While on the Pincio, don't miss the recently restored  **Orologio ad Acqua,** a whimsical 19th-century water clock in a delightful little pond.

Open Sunday only (10am–2pm), the Renaissance  **Gardens at Villa Medici** comprise the open-air home of priceless works of ancient sculpture. In his *Italian Hours,* Henry James called the exclusive gardens "the most enchanting place." Walk back to Porta Pinciana.

A view up Viale del Museo Borghese.

Appia Antica (Appian Way)

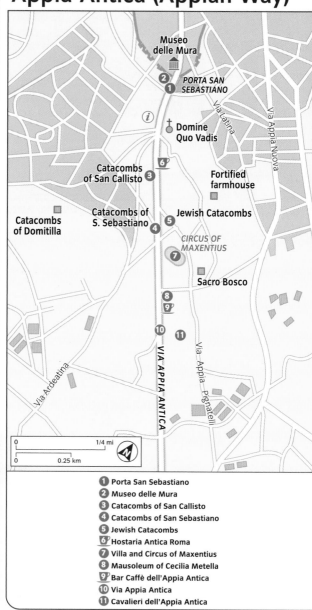

1. Porta San Sebastiano
2. Museo delle Mura
3. Catacombs of San Callisto
4. Catacombs of San Sebastiano
5. Jewish Catacombs
6. Hostaria Antica Roma
7. Villa and Circus of Maxentius
8. Mausoleum of Cecilia Metella
9. Bar Caffè dell'Appia Antica
10. Via Appia Antica
11. Cavalieri dell'Appia Antica

The most important of Rome's famous ancient roads, the rustic Appian Way (Via Appia Antica) is home to most of the city's catacombs and a world away from the bustle of the *centro*. Visit the catacombs for a fascinating descent into the ancient tufa tunnels where Roman Christians were buried, then continue south to the Circus of Maxentius and Tomb of Cecilia Metella, where a landscape steeped in antiquity should leave you spellbound. **Bus: 118 (from Metro Circo Massimo or Metro Piramide) to the Porta San Sebastiano stop. Or, if you start at the catacombs, take bus 118 to either the Catacombe San Callisto (see bullet ③) or Basilica San Sebastiano (see bullet ④). Or take a taxi (10–15 min. from the city center; 15€–20€). Allow 3 to 4 hours for the trip.**

The massive ❶ **Porta San Sebastiano,** a brick gateway left over from Rome's 3rd-century-A.D. fortification, marks the start of Via Appia Antica's southbound route. Inside the gateway is the ❷ **Museo delle Mura,** (Museum of the Walls), which has neat exhibits on ancient Roman defense systems. Restoration permitting, you can also walk on top of a stretch of wall here for an impressive view of the countryside. *Via di Porta di San Sebastiano 18.* ☎ *06-70475284. Tues–Sun 9am–7pm (until 5pm Nov–Mar).*

The next mile of the Appia is visually underwhelming and plagued with traffic; take bus 118 five stops (about 1.6km/1 mile) south to the catacombs, where the landscape is greener and quieter.

A well-preserved, painted family tomb in the catacombs.

Enjoy Rome offers a 3-hour bus and walking tour of the Appia Antica, including the stupendous aqueduct park off Via Appia Nuova, otherwise hard to reach. *Call for tour times.* ☎ *06-4451843.*

Skip the package-tour-infested catacombs of Domitilla and make for San Callisto or San Sebastiano instead (below). Admission to each catacomb (6€ adults, 3€ ages 3–15) includes a 35-minute guided tour, offered in English every 15 minutes or so. The tours can be quite large and guides' accents difficult to understand, so try to stay close to the front of the group.

❸ **Catacombs of San Callisto.** Once home to 500,000 tombs, these are by far the most impressive and extensive of Rome's catacombs. *Via Appia Antica 110–126. Thurs–Tues 8:30am–noon, 2:30–5pm. Closed Feb.*

❹ **Catacombs of San Sebastiano.** A 5-minute walk from San Callisto, and more intimate than San Callisto, with better-preserved tomb decorations, this cluster of pagan tombs offers a fascinating look at the typically Roman practice of layering architectures and faiths. *Via Appia Antica 136. Mon–Sat 8:30am–noon, 2:30–5pm. Closed mid-Nov to mid-Dec.*

The Circus of Maxentius.

While catacombs are most often associated with Christianity, the Jews of ancient Rome also buried their dead in the same kinds of underground networks. The ⑤ **Jewish Catacombs** at Via Appia Antica 119A can be visited only with prior permission from the Cultural Heritage Department. ☎ 06-67103819. Fax 06-6892115.

⑥ **Hostaria Antica Roma.** After the catacombs, enjoy a relaxed and rustic meal as you sit in the shade of trees, umbrellas, and a 1st-century-B.C. columbarium (funerary monument with niches for the deceaseds' ashes). Wonderful Roman atmosphere and hospitality abound. *Via*

Appia Antica 87. ☎ *06-5132888. www.anticaroma.it. Closed Mon. $$–$$$.*

⑦ **Villa and Circus of Maxentius.** A 5-minute walk south of San Sebastiano, the ruins of a 4th-century imperial country estate (poorly preserved) and circus (chariot racetrack, which held 10,000 spectators) lie in a field on the east side of the ancient road. Pay the small entrance fee here for awe-inspiring views of Cecilia Metella among the umbrella pines, and for a closer look at the circus's construction. *Via Appia Antica 153. Tues–Fri, Sun 9am–1:30pm; Sat 9am–1 hr. before sunset.*

Visiting the Catacombs

Ancient Roman law forbade burials, regardless of religion, inside the city walls. Of the more than 60 catacombs that have been discovered on the roads leading out of Rome, the most famous are San Callisto and San Sebastiano on the Appian Way (see bullets ③ and ④). On your guided visit, you'll descend through multiple levels of 1,900-year-old hand-dug corridors, past a mind-boggling number of tomb niches. (To protect them from looters, the bones have been removed.) Christian-themed inscriptions and frescoes, often endearingly simplistic but carrying strong messages of faith, are everywhere in the catacombs.

8 Mausoleum of Cecilia Metella. The best view of this cylindrical tomb of a 1st-century-B.C. socialite is from the middle of the Circus of Maxentius (above) or the road. (The entrance fee here does not gain you access to the tomb's interior but to a courtyard cluttered with ancient marble pieces.) The Appian Way was the Rodeo Drive of tombs in antiquity, and Cecilia Metella's was only one of hundreds of marble-clad sepulchers that used to crowd the roadside. The other tombs, dismantled by the popes and barbarians in the Middle Ages for their valuable materials, are now little more than brick stumps. *Via Appia Antica 161. Tues–Sun 9am–1 hr. before sunset.*

☕ **Bar Caffè dell'Appia Antica.** A bike ride can be a very pleasant way to see the Appia Antica, provided you start here and ride south, where vehicle traffic is light to non-existent. This informal coffee bar rents bikes by the hour. The Appian Way's flagstones can get very uneven at times, meaning you'll have to get off and walk a bit, but you can travel as far as 3km (2 miles) on the ancient road, viewing ruins and rural life, and not worry about getting lost—the Appia's path is due south and dead-straight. *Via Appia Antica 175. $.*

10 Via Appia Antica. The leafy, 3km (2-mile) segment beginning at Cecilia Metella is the Appia at its most evocative. Here, the road is 4m (14 ft.) wide (the Roman standard), with ancient basalt flagstones still in place. Private villas on either side of the road eventually give way to ruins-strewn fields and the occasional flock of sheep. You'll need to walk for at least 500m (⅓ mile) to appreciate the change of scenery; beyond that, it's somewhat repetitive—umbrella pines, tomb stumps—but still wonderfully soaked in history. *Public transportation is spotty at the southern end of the road; return by foot or bike to 8. From there, catch bus no. 660 to Metro San Giovanni, or call a taxi (☎ 06-3570) from the bar.*

11 Cavalieri dell'Appia Antica. If you really want to do as the Romans did on the "Queen of Roads," get a horse! This small, friendly stable offers an alternative to biking and walking on the Appia Antica. Scenic rides (for all skill levels) take you past the most important ruins. *Via dei Cercenii 15. ☎ 06-7801214 or 328-2085787. 20€ per 1-hr. ride. Owners speak almost no English, so have your hotel make reservations for you. Tues–Sun 10am–6pm. Bus: 118.*

Travelers stroll or take a break on the pastoral Appian Way.

Other Rome **Parks to Explore**

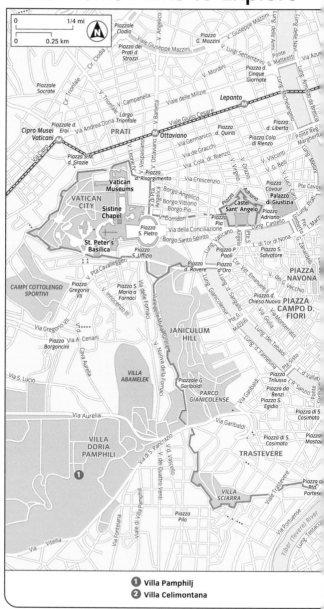

1 Villa Pamphilj
2 Villa Celimontana

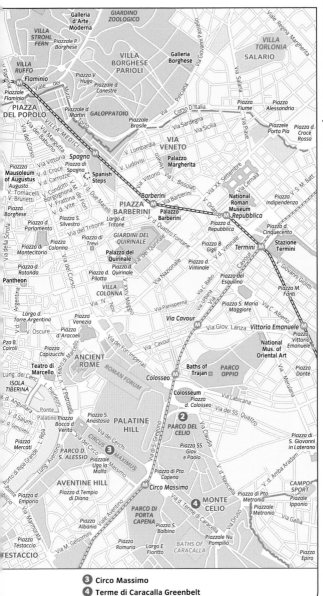

3 Circo Massimo

4 Terme di Caracalla Greenbelt

In addition to the parks and green areas I've mentioned so far in this chapter, other parks I love are Villa Pamphilj, a tourist-free and gargantuan sprawl of woods, lawns, and manicured gardens west of Trastevere; and Villa Celimontana, a beautiful hilltop park a stone's throw from the Colosseum. Circo Massimo and the Terme di Caracalla greenbelt offer runners the chance to work out alongside majestic ruins.

❶ Villa Pamphilj. This huge swath of green (184 hectares/455 acres) is where Romans come when they don't want to slum it with tourists at Villa Borghese. Its hilly topography is best suited for serious joggers, but Villa Pamphilj has no shortage of scenic trails for walkers in search of *bel respiro* ("good breathing," the original name of the 17th-c. park). Locals love to bring full-spread picnics here on weekends. A delightful pond teeming with turtles awaits the leftovers. *Bus: 44, 175, or 870.*

❷ Villa Celimontana. Perched atop Celio Hill, just a 5-minute walk south of the Colosseum, the Villa Celimontana park has a bustling kids' play area, limited jogging paths, and a fabulous nighttime jazz festival in summer, where the setting is straight out of *La Dolce Vita*. *Metro: Colosseo. Bus: 60, 75, 81, 175, or 271. Tram: 3.*

❸ Circo Massimo. Many ridicule the derelict state of the Circus Maximus, Rome's erstwhile racetrack, but there's still something glorious about treading the same earth where chariots once thundered, to the deafening cheers of 300,000 Roman spectators, under the imperial auspices of Palatine Hill. Palatine Hill is where the emperors lived, and the slope you see from here is the spot from which the emperors watched the races. See how fast you can complete some laps (one lap is 1,200m/¾ mile), the standard distance for all ancient races. There's no shade, however, and you'll need to watch out for broken beer bottles. *Metro: Circo Massimo. Bus: 30, 60, 75, 170, 175. or 271. Tram: 3.*

❹ Terme di Caracalla Greenbelt. "Real" Roman runners eschew the Circus Maximus, but you will find them treading the shaded paths just to the south, near the 3rd-century ruins of the Baths of Caracalla. The grassy areas here are also perfect for doing pushups and sit-ups—or yoga, if you can tune out the traffic. ●

The Snake Fountain at Villa Pamphilj.

Rome's ancient chariot racetrack, the Circo Massimo.

6 The Best **Dining**

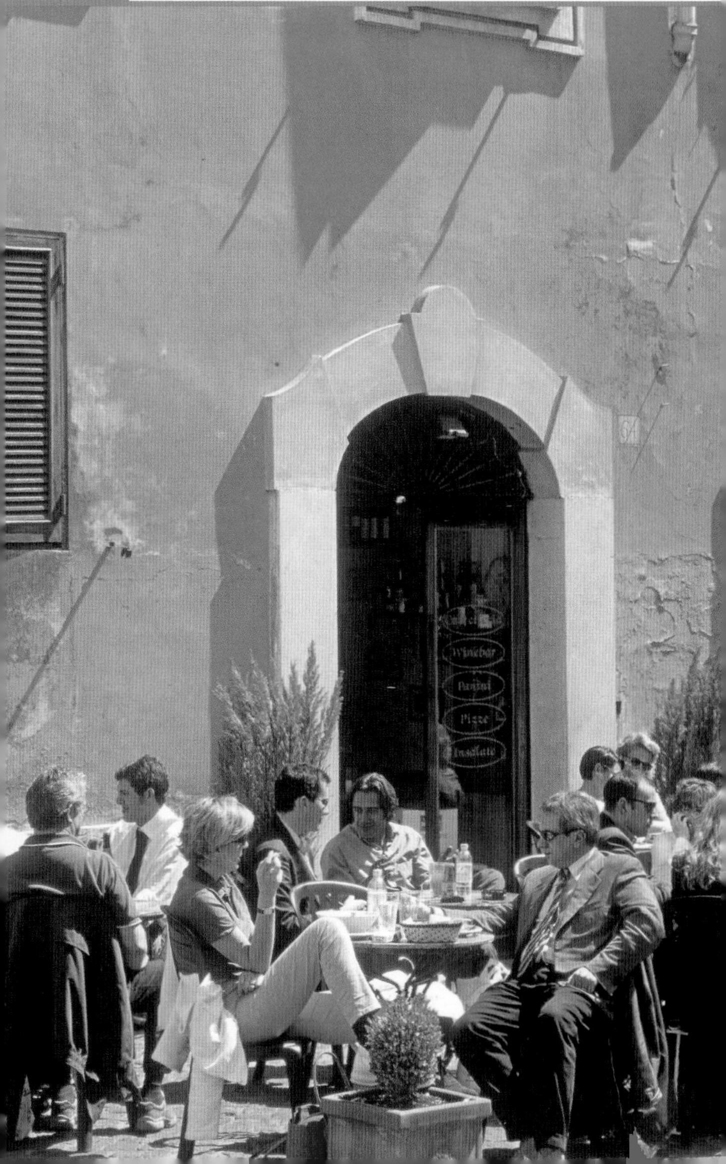

Dining Best Bets

Best **All-Around** *Cucina Romana* **Experience**
★★ Perilli $$ *Via Marmorata 39* (p 113)

Best **Understatedly Cool, Insider Spots**
★★ Maccheroni $$ *Via delle Coppelle 44 (p 112);* and ★★ Fiaschetteria Beltramme $$ *Via della Croce 39 (p 109)*

Best **Boisterous Lunch**
★★ Enoteca Corsi $ *Via del Gesù 87 (p 109)*

Best **Pizzeria**
★★ La Montecarlo $ *Vicolo Savelli 11 (p 111)*

Best **Outdoor Tables**
★★ Antica Pesa $$$ *Via Garibaldi 18 (p 108);* and ★★ La Veranda $$$ *Borgo Santo Spirito 73 (p 111)*

Best **For Serious Oenophiles and Food Snobs**
★★ Casa Bleve $$ *Via del Teatro Pace 48-49 (p 108);* and ★★ Enoteca Cavour 313 $$ *Via Cavour 313 (p 109)*

Best **Bragging-Rights Splurge**
★★★ La Pergola $$$$ *Via Cadlolo 101 (p 111)*

Best **Paparazzi Haunt**
★★ Due Ladroni $$$ *Piazza Nicosia 24 (p 109)*

Best **Quick Lunch Near the Ruins**
★ La Bottega del Caffè $ *Piazza Madonna dei Monti 5 (p 110)*

Best **Coffee**
★★★ Bar Sant'Eustachio $ *Piazza di Sant'Eustachio 82 (p 108)*

Best **Seafood**
★★★ Quinzi e Gabrieli $$$$ *Via delle Coppelle 5 (p 113)*

Dining Tips

In this chapter, I've given you my top recommendations for different cuisine types, price ranges, and levels of formality. However, should you strike out on your own, keep these guidelines in mind:

1. Don't eat at any restaurant where the menu is translated into five languages (or, worse yet, where the menu is simply photographs of spaghetti drowning in red sauce).
2. Avoid restaurants where the waitstaff is overly solicitous of passers-by. If their restaurant is so great, why do they need to hustle you in off the street?
3. Most restaurants located right on the main piazzas are big-time tourist traps. Stick to the smaller squares and side streets.
4. Do as the Romans do. If you follow the locals (they're the ones who go out after 8pm), you'll be in good shape.
5. Never order priced-by-weight seafood without first confirming what it will actually cost. That baked turbot might come back to haunt you once you see the insane 100€ charge for it on your bill.

Previous page: Enjoying the sunshine at an outdoor cafe in Rome.

Centro Storico Dining

Bar Sant'Eustachio 9	La Montecarlo 3
Casa Bleve 8	Maccheroni 11
Cul de Sac 4	Osteria del Gallo 1
Hostaria Romanesca 6	Pierluigi 2
Il Bacaro 12	Quinzi e Gabrieli 10
Insalata Ricca 7	Taverna del Campo 5

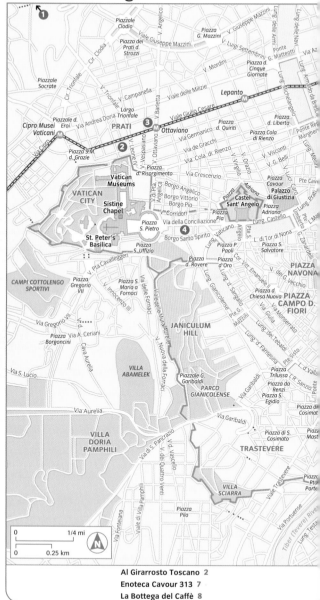

Al Girarrosto Toscano **2**

Enoteca Cavour 313 **7**

La Bottega del Caffè **8**

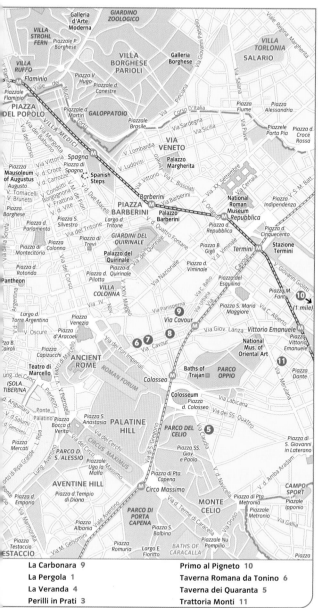

Tridente/Via Veneto Dining

Due Ladroni **4**

Enoteca Antica di Via della Croce **2**

Enoteca Corsi **5**

Fiaschetteria Beltramme **3**

'Gusto **1**

Trastevere Dining

Antica Pesa 3

Dar Poeta 2

Osteria der Belli 4

Ponte Sisto 1

Spirito di Vino 5

Testaccio Dining

Checchino dal 1887 3

Da Bucatino 1

Perilli 2

Rome Restaurants A to Z

★★ Al Girarrosto Toscano VATICAN *GRILL* Carnivores go wild for the succulent perfection of these Tuscan-style grilled meats. *Via Germanico 58–60 (at Via Vespasiano).* ☎ 06-39723373. *Entrees 10€–20€. AE, MC, V. Open Tues–Sun lunch and dinner. Metro: Ottaviano. Bus: 23 or 492. Tram: 19. Map p 104.*

★★ Antica Pesa TRASTEVERE *ROMAN* Refined *signori e signore* trek halfway up the Gianicolo Hill to this charmer with a reliable, traditional menu and lovely interior garden—a converted bocce court. *Via Garibaldi 18 (at Via del Mattonato).* ☎ 06-5809236. *Entrees 12€–20€. AE, MC, V. Open Mon–Sat 7:30–11pm. Bus: 23, 271, or 280. Map p 107.*

★★★ Bar Sant'Eustachio PANTHEON *COFFEE* Its blue-script neon sign is a beacon for coffee snobs in search of the richest, creamiest brew in the city. The *gran caffè* is the specialty. *Piazza Sant'Eustachio 82 (south side of square).* ☎ 06-6561309. *Coffee 1.50€–4€. No credit cards. Open daily 8:30am–1am. Bus: 30, 40, 62, 64, 70, 87, 116, or 492. Map p 103.*

★★ Casa Bleve PANTHEON *WINE BAR* Lavish spreads of cheeses, meats, olives, and other delicacies at this ambitious *enoteca*-and-more resemble a Renaissance feast. And there's a vaulted and columned room to match. *Via del Teatro Valle 48–49 (off Corso Vittorio Emanuele II).* ☎ 06-6865970. www.casableve.it. *Entrees 8€–18€. AE, MC, V. Open Tues–Sat for lunch and dinner. Bus: 30, 40, 62, 64, 70, 87, 116, or 492. Tram: 8. Map p 103.*

★★★ Checchino dal 1887 TESTACCIO *ROMAN* Often mischaracterized as an offal-only joint, this

establishment, opened in 1887 across from Rome's now-defunct abattoir, is a special-night-out type of place, serving wonderful *bucatini all'amatriciana* and veal saltimbocca—as well as hearty plates of, er, heart and other slaughterhouse cast-offs. Tasting menus from 42€. *Via di Monte Testaccio 30 (at Via Galvani).* ☎ 06-5746318. *www.checchino-dal-1887.com. Entrees 16€–30€. AE, MC, V. Open Tues–Sat for dinner. Metro: Piramide. Bus: 23, 95, 170, or 280. Tram: 3. Map p 107.*

★ Cul de Sac PIAZZA NAVONA *WINE BAR* Cozy and lively, this popular *enoteca* has a mind-boggling selection of cheeses and cold cuts, savory Mediterranean salads and hors d'oeuvres, and wines by the glass or bottle. *Piazza Pasquino 73 (at Via del Governo Vecchio).* ☎ 06-68801094. *Entrees 8€–13€. MC, V. Open Tues–Sun for lunch, daily for dinner. Bus: 40, 62, 64, 70, 87, or 492. Map p 103.*

★★ Da Bucatino TESTACCIO *ROMAN* The best place in Testaccio for a casual Roman meal, this authentic *hostaria* treats you like

The charming facade of the restaurant Checchino dal 1887.

family, and you'll get to watch the antics of the many local families—from *nonna* to *bambino*—that eat here regularly. *Via Luca della Robbia 84–86 (at Via Bodoni).* ☎ *06-5746886. Entrees 7€–15€. AE, MC, V. Open Tues–Sun for lunch and dinner. Bus: 23, 75, 271, or 280. Tram 3. Map p 107.*

★★ **Dar Poeta** TRASTEVERE *PIZZA* Throw carb-caution to the wind at this hard-to-find, eternally packed pizzeria. Expect a wait, then gorge yourself on flavor-filled *bruschette* and pizzas, but save room for the heavenly Nutella-and-ricotta dessert calzone. *Vicolo del Bologna 45 (at Piazza della Scala).* ☎ *06-5880516. Pizzas 8€–12€. AE, MC, V. Open daily for dinner only. Bus: 23, 271, or 280. Map p 107.*

★★ **Due Ladroni** PIAZZA DEL POPOLO *ITALIAN* Italian gossip mags always feature a few grainy photos of celebs dining at this classy but unpretentious restaurant, where standard fare is solid, and waiters have the tip-enhancing quality of treating you as if you might be famous. *Piazza Nicosia 24 (off Via di Ripetta).* ☎ *06-6896299. Entrees 14€–24€. AE, MC, V. Open Mon–Sat for lunch and dinner. Bus: 87, 280, 492, or 628. Map p 106.*

★ **Enoteca Antica di Via della Croce** SPANISH STEPS *WINE BAR* A prime spot to rest your feet after shopping around the Spanish Steps. There's a long bar, as well as table service in back and outside, great antipasti, and dozens of wines by the glass. *Via della Croce 76b (at Via Bocca di Leone).* ☎ *06-6790896. Entrees 10€–16€. AE, MC, V. Open daily for lunch and dinner. Metro: Spagna. Map p 106.*

★★ **Enoteca Cavour 313** MONTI *WINE BAR* Serious foodies stop into this handsome gem near the Forum for plates of the highest-quality

Patrons enjoying pizza and drinks at Dar Poeta in Trastevere.

prosciutto, carpaccio, cheese, vegetable dishes, and, of course, wine. *Via Cavour 313 (at Via dell'Agnello).* ☎ *06-6785496. Entrees 10€–18€. AE, MC, V. Open daily for lunch and dinner. Closed Sun Jun–Aug. Metro: Cavour or Colosseo. Bus: 75, 85, 87, 175, 571. Map p 104.*

★★ **Enoteca Corsi** PANTHEON *ROMAN* At this terrific remnant of early-20th-century Rome, government office workers settle into cramped tables to eat hearty, messy plates like *amatriciana,* which sloshes dangerously close to their Zegna ties and Armani shirts. The loud and lively scene—and the prices—are a time warp back to more carefree days. *Via del Gesù 87 (near Via del Plebiscito).* ☎ *06-6790821. Entrees 7€–12€. MC, V. Open Mon–Sat for lunch only. Bus: 30, 40, 62, 64, 87, 492, 571. Map p 106.*

★★ **Fiaschetteria Beltramme** SPANISH STEPS *ROMAN* Chic locals, expats, and visitors in-the-know brave the no-phone, no-reservations policy at this homey spot, run by cool women, for one of the most satisfying casual-dining experiences in the *centro.* The menu offers a nice mix of cold, lighter plates and traditional Roman dishes—their *carbonara* is outstanding. A few communal tables

Platter of traditional Roman antipasto.

accommodate solo diners. *Via della Croce 39 (at Via Belsiana). No phone. Entrees 10€–18€. No credit cards. Open Mon–Sat for lunch and dinner. Metro: Spagna. Map p 106.*

★ **'Gusto** PIAZZA DEL POPOLO *CREATIVE ITALIAN/PIZZA* This conglomerate of hip, modern restaurants has several locations on a Fascist-era piazza. The pizzeria (at no. 9) is buzzy and kid-friendly; the new "fish and vegetables" restaurant (at no. 28) is fresh and airy, with two whitewashed dining levels and fantastic, unique pastas. Traditionalists may not like the 'Gusto phenomenon, but it's one of few places in Rome besides McDonald's where you can have a sit-down meal any time of day. *Piazza Augusto Imperatore 7, 9, and 28, Via della Frezza 16.* ☎ *06-3226273. www.gusto.it. Entrees 8€–22€. AE, MC, V. Open daily; hours vary by location. Metro: Flaminio or Spagna. Bus: 913. Map p 106.*

Hostaria Romanesca CAMPO DE' FIORI *ROMAN* Recommended mostly for its ringside seats on the piazza, Romanesca does dependable Roman fare at low prices, including a gloriously juicy *pollo e peperoni* (stewed chicken with peppers) for 8€. *Campo de' Fiori 40 (east side of square).* ☎ *06-6864024. Entrees 7€–12€. No credit cards. Open Tues–Sun for lunch and dinner. Bus: 30, 40, 62, 64, 70, 87, 116, 492, or 571. Tram: 8. Map p 103.*

★★ **Il Bacaro** PANTHEON *ITALIAN* When you want to escape the chaos of central Rome, this romantic and low-key spot on a hidden back street offers respite from the traffic and tourist crush. Insanely delicious *primi* and *secondi* (like *tortelli* with taleggio and pumpkin, or grouper with porcini mushrooms) are a welcome departure from strictly traditional Roman fare. *Via degli Spagnoli 27 (off Via della Scrofa).* ☎ *06-6872554. www.ilbacaro.com. Entrees 12€–21€. AE, MC, V. Open Mon–Sat for lunch and dinner. Bus: 30, 62, 70, 81, 87, 116, or 492. Map p 103.*

★ **Insalata Ricca** CAMPO DE' FIORI *SALADS* The "rich salads" at this wildly popular lunch spot are laden with everything from lobster meat to hearts of palm to fresh mozzarella. Other branches around town are no match for the original. *Largo Chiavari 85 (at Corso Vittorio Emanuele II).* ☎ *06-68803656. www.linsalataricca. it. Entrees 9€–16€. AE, MC, V. Open daily for lunch and dinner. Bus: 30, 40, 62, 64, 70, 87, 116, 492, or 571. Tram: 8. Map p 103.*

★ **La Bottega del Caffè** MONTI *LIGHT FARE/PIZZA* The social epicenter of newly hip Monti has tons of outdoor tables and a laid-back vibe—no one cares whether you order a full meal (there's everything from salads to pizzas) or just a cappuccino. Perfect for lunch between tours of ruins, or for a late-night bite after hitting the bars in the area. *Piazza Madonna dei Monti 5 (at Via dei Serpenti).* ☎ *393-9311013. Entrees 7€–14€. AE, MC, V. Open daily for lunch and dinner. Metro: Cavour. Bus: 60, 75, 85, 87, or 175. Map p 104.*

★★ **La Carbonara** MONTI *ROMAN/PIZZA* Not to be confused with the touristy La Carbonara on Campo de' Fiori, this hip and buzzy trattoria (with exposed brick vaults, and white walls that patrons are welcome to write on) has a sprawling menu of everything Roman—all prepared with love and aplomb by *mamma* Teresa. For a place this down-to-earth, there's an extensive (and well-priced) wine list. *Via Panisperna 214 (near Via Cimarra).* ☎ *06-4825176. www.lacarbonara.it. Entrees 9€–16€. AE, MC, V. Open Mon–Sat for lunch and dinner. Metro: Cavour. Bus: 40, 60, 62, 64, 75. Map p 104.*

★★ **La Montecarlo** PIAZZA NAVONA *PIZZA* Dirt-cheap and immensely popular with real Romans, Montecarlo feels like a big party: Efficient, flirtatious servers sling piping-hot, thin-crusted pies on metal pans, and the wine and beer flow freely. *Vicolo Savelli 11 (at Corso Vittorio Emanuele II).* ☎ *06-*

6861877. Pizzas 6€–10€. AE, MC, V. Open Tues–Sun for lunch and dinner. Bus: 40, 64, or 571. Map p 103.

★★★ **La Pergola** MONTE MARIO/WESTERN SUBURBS *MEDITERRANEAN* Celebrity chef Heinz Beck's always-perfect, creative cuisine employs the full bounty of the region, from fish to seasonal vegetables to rare fowl and game. Complemented by dramatic views, good-looking staff, and two Michelin stars, this is one of the best meals you'll have in your life—and it's priced accordingly. Jacket required. *Via Cadlolo 101 (at the Cavalieri Hilton).* ☎ *06-35092211. Reserve at least 1 month in advance. 100€ and up per person. AE, MC, V. Open Tues–Sat for dinner only; closed part of Jan and Aug. Map p 104.*

★★ **La Veranda** VATICAN *CREATIVE ITALIAN* A gorgeous frescoed hall gives way to leafy terraces at this wonderfully patinated place, a favorite of the Vatican press corps and visiting cardinals. On the menu, look for inventive dishes like *tonnarelli* with ricotta and cinnamon. *Borgo Santo Spirito 73 (at the Hotel Columbus).* ☎ *06-6872973. Entrees 13€–28€. AE, MC, V. Open daily for lunch and dinner. Bus: 23, 40, 62, 64, or 271. Map p 104.*

Typical Roman formaggio (cheese) shop.

★★ Maccheroni PANTHEON
ITALIAN Popular with Roman scenesters, this trendy spot is also one of the best dining values in Rome, offering simple but perfectly executed dishes (like pasta *all'amatriciana* and chicken *alla cacciatora*) at humane prices. *Via delle Coppelle 44 (at Via degli Spagnoli).* ☎ 06-68307895. www.ristorantemaccheroni.com. *Entrees 10€–16€. AE, MC, V. Open daily for lunch and dinner. Bus: 30, 62, 70, 81, 87, 116, or 492. Map p 103.*

★ Osteria del Gallo PIAZZA NAVONA *ITALIAN* This lovely little trat, on a quiet *centro storico* alley, was made for languorous lunching. Menu standouts include the pecorino cheese plate with fig marmalade, and the ravioli with porcini. *Vicolo di Montevecchio 27 (at Via della Pace).* ☎ 06/6873781. *Entrees 10€–18€. AE, MC, V. Open Mon–Sat for dinner, Tues–Sun for lunch. Bus: 30, 70, 87, or 492. Map p 103.*

★ Osteria der Belli TRASTEVERE *SARDINIAN/SEAFOOD* Proprietor Leo keeps locals and visitors alike happy with a knock-out sauté of clams and mussels, *spaghetti alla pescatora*, and grilled swordfish. The energetic indoor-outdoor spot gets especially lively on Friday nights, when boozy old-timers settle in for their fish fix. *Piazza Sant'Apollonia 9–11 (at Via della Lungaretta).* ☎ 06-5803782. *Entrees 9€–15€. AE, MC, V. Open Tues–Sun for lunch and dinner. Bus: 23, 271, 280, 780, or H. Tram: 8. Map p 107.*

Snacking as the Romans Do— and Saving Money

Most locals don't eat full sit-down meals at lunch and dinner; you can save a bunch of euros by following their lead.

Panini & Pizza Instead of Lunch

Any time of day, grab a savory *pizza farcita* (pizza bread sandwich stuffed with your choice of veggies, cheeses, or meats) from **Aristocampo** (Campo de' Fiori 30; open daily late), **Frontoni** (Viale Trastevere 52, closed Sun), or **Burro e Alici** (Via della Mercede 34, near the Spanish Steps; open daily), or squares of pizza at any *pizza al taglio* joint that smells good (I like **Panificio Renella,** at Via del Moro 15/16 in Trastevere, but there are fine spots all over town). Most of these places have some sort of seating—when in Rome, resting your feet is essential! For a more bare-bones experience, any *alimentari* (grocer's) will make you a simple panino for around 2.50€. Take it to Villa Borghese, or to a grassy site like the Palatine or Baths of Caracalla, for a picnic later in the day.

Aperitivo Instead of Dinner

Come sundown, it's *aperitivo* time (happy hour) at most Roman bars and lounges; that means a free buffet of tasty Italian specialties for anyone who buys a drink. In other words, an 8€ prosecco entitles you to a whole dinner's worth of food—and no one frowns upon going back for seconds and thirds!

The classic recipe for carbonara, a quintessentially Roman pasta sauce, includes eggs, pancetta, and pecorino cheese.

★★ Perilli TESTACCIO *ROMAN*
Step back in time and enjoy the old-school atmosphere at this beloved institution of Roman *ristorazione*. With zero pretense, Perilli's formally attired waitstaff treat you with the right amount of informality and serve you unadulterated renditions of Roman classics. Going to Perilli is an event, like a play with many acts, so you really *should* get the *antipasto*, *primo*, *secondo*, and *dolce*, or you'll be missing out on the full experience. *Via Marmorata 39 (at Via Galvani).* ☎ *06-5742415. Entrees 9€–16€. AE, MC, V. Open Thurs–Tues for lunch and dinner. Reservations recommended. Bus: 23, 75, 95, 170, or 280. Tram: 3. Map p 107.*

★ Perilli in Prati VATICAN *ROMAN*
An excellent alternative to the tourist-trap eateries that plague the Vatican area, this family-run trat (it's the younger, quieter relative of Perilli in Testaccio) offers spot-on renditions of Roman classics like *gricia* pasta (with pig cheek, sheep's cheese, and pepper) and warm service. *Via Otranto 9–11 (at Viale Giulio Cesare).* ☎ *06-3700156. www.perilliinprati.it. Entrees 9€–16€. AE, MC, V. Open Mon–Fri for lunch and dinner, Sat for dinner only. Metro: Ottaviano. Bus: 23. Tram: 19. Map p 104.*

★ Pierluigi CAMPO DE' FIORI
ITALIAN Popular with older, well-heeled locals and tourists, this trusty indoor-outdoor trat does a mean octopus *soppressata* and *tagliata di manzo* (tender beef strips on a bed of rucola). *Piazza de' Ricci 144 (at Via Monserrato).* ☎ *06-6861302. Entrees 10€–20€. AE, MC, V. Open Tues–Sun for lunch and dinner. Bus: 23, 40, 64, 116, 271, 280, or 571. Map p 103.*

★ Ponte Sisto TRASTEVERE
ITALIAN/SEAFOOD With long, communal tables and red-check tablecloths, this bustling and well-priced joint, with its generous portions of Neapolitan fare, is great for groups. *Via di Ponte Sisto 80 (at Piazza Trilussa).* ☎ *06-5883411. Entrees 8€–14€. AE, MC, V. Open daily for lunch and dinner. Bus: 23, 271, or 280. Map p 107.*

★★ Primo al Pigneto
PIGNETO/EASTERN SUBURBS *NEW ITALIAN* The hot address for new (and healthier) Roman cuisine in Rome's gritty-but-ever-gentrifying "it" neighborhood. The talented young chef, Marco Gallotta, prepares inventive and light fare, with superior-quality ingredients (veggies, meats, cheese, seafood) that are never overly processed. The stylish space features lots of metal and glass and is open from breakfast to late night—you're welcome to stop in even for an antipasto and glass of wine almost anytime. *Via del Pigneto 46 (near Via Giovanni de Agostini).* ☎ *06-7013827. www.primoalpigneto.it. Entrees 10€–18€. AE, MC, V. Open Tues–Sun all day. Bus: 81. Map p 104.*

★★★ Quinzi e Gabrieli PANTHEON *SEAFOOD* Local VIPs and visiting movie stars come here for the absolute best (and most expensive) seafood pastas and entrees in town. Lunch tasting menus are a bit easier on the wallet. *Via delle Coppelle 5 (at Via degli Spagnoli).* ☎ *06-6879389. www.quinziegabrieli.it.*

Gelato lovers on a Rome street.

Entrees 20€–35€. AE, MC, V. Open Mon–Sat for lunch and dinner. Bus: 30, 70, 87, 116, or 492. Map p 103.

★★ **Spirito di Vino** TRASTEVERE *ROMAN* In a medieval synagogue atop a 2nd-century-street, the Catalani family does exceptional modern and ancient Roman cuisine (like *maiale alla mazio,* a favorite pork dish of Julius Caesar's) and other plates as warm and comforting as the ambience. *Via dei Genovesi 31 (at Vicolo dell'Atleta).* ☎ *06-5896689. Entrees 15€–24€. AE, MC, V. Open Mon–Sat for dinner only. Bus: 23, 271, 280, 780, or H. Tram: 8. Map p 107.*

★ **Taverna dei Quaranta** ANCIENT ROME *ROMAN* Honest eats a stone's throw from the Colosseum, with a mostly local clientele. The staff is super-friendly and the kitchen is fairly sophisticated, frequently offering regional menus of hard-to-find pastas and other specialties. Pizza served at dinner only. *Via Claudia 24 (at Via Annia).* ☎ *06-7000550. Entrees 9€–15€. AE, MC, V. Open Tues–Sun for lunch and dinner. Metro: Colosseo. Bus: 75, 81, 175. Tram: 3. Map p 104.*

★ **Taverna del Campo** CAMPO DE' FIORI *CAFE/WINE BAR* This trendy lunch and *aperitivo* spot on Campo de' Fiori has terrific, garlicky sandwiches, cheap cocktails and *vino* by the glass, and free peanuts. Snag a front-row table, don your fashionista sunglasses, and watch the pageant go by. *Campo de' Fiori 16 (at Via dei Baullari).* ☎ *06-6874402. Sandwiches 4.50€–6€. No credit cards. Open Tues–Sun 8am–1am. Bus: 30, 40, 62, 64, 70, 87, 492, or 571. Map p 103.*

★ **Taverna Romana da Tonino** MONTI *ROMAN* Sink your teeth into succulent roast lamb and other hearty *secondi* at this inexpensive, homey trat near the Forum. Come early or be prepared to wait. *Via Madonna dei Monti 79 (at Via dell' Agnello).* ☎ *06-4745325. Entrees 8€–14€. No credit cards. Open Mon–Sat for lunch and dinner. Metro: Cavour. Bus: 60, 75, 85, 87, or 175. Map p 104.*

★★ **Trattoria Monti** ESQUILINO *REGIONAL/MARCHE* This cozy trat run by the earnest (and very good-looking) Camerucci family serves outstanding, hearty pastas and meat dishes from the Marche region. Don't miss the *tortino di parmigiano* dessert. *Via di San Vito 13A (at Via Merulana).* ☎ *06-4466573. Entrees 10€–18€. AE, MC, V. Open Tues–Sat for dinner, Sun lunch only. Metro: Vittorio. Bus: 714. Map p 104.* ●

Nightlife Best Bets

Best Bar for Getting Wasted
on 3€ Glasses of Wine
★★ Vineria Reggio, *Campo de' Fiori
15 (p 122)*

Best for Hanging with the
International In-Crowd
★★ Salotto 42, *Piazza di Pietra 42
(p 122)*

Most Romantic
★★ Casina Valadier, *Piazza
Bucarest (p 121)*

Best Pub
★★ Cork's Inn, *Via delle Tre Can-
nelle 8 (p 124);* and ★ Fiddler's
Elbow, *Via dell'Olmata 43 (p 124)*

Best Aperitivo
★★ Société Lutèce, *Piazza Montevecchio 17 (p 122);* and ★★ Freni
e Frizione, *Via del Politeama 4–6
(p 121)*

Best People-Watching
★★ Antico Caffè della Pace, *Via
della Pace (p 121)*

Best Summer Party
La Terrazza dell'Eur, *Piazzale
Kennedy (p 124)*

Best Intimate Alfresco Spot
★★ Le Coppelle 52, *Piazza delle
Coppelle 52 (p 121)*

Best Club-Hopping Zone
Testaccio and Ostiense

Best Live Music
★★★ Big Mama, *Vicolo di San
Francesco a Ripa 18 (p 123)*

Best Gay Disco
★★ Alibi, *Via di Monte Testaccio
40–47 (p 123)*

The nightspot Freni e Frizioni.

*Previous page: A belltower of the church of Trinità dei Monti, looking over the Spanish
Steps to Roman rooftops.*

Centro Storico Nightlife

Antico Caffè della Pace 4	Le Coppelle 52 5
Bartaruga 10	Portal 2
Casina Valadier 1	Salotto 42 6
Cork's Inn 9	Société Lutèce 3
Freni e Frizioni 11	Taverna del Campo 7
Isola del Cinema 12	Vineria Reggio 8

Rome Nightlife

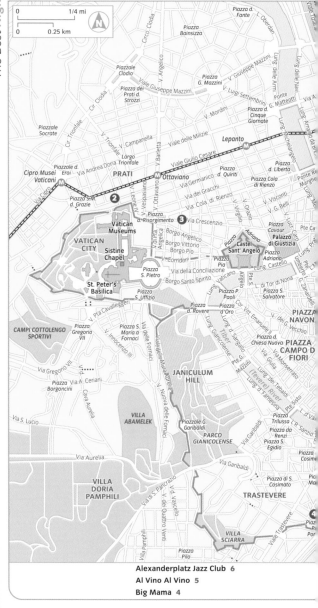

Alexanderplatz Jazz Club 6
Al Vino Al Vino 5
Big Mama 4

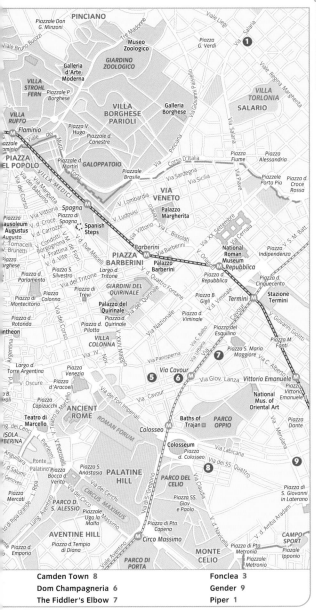

Testaccio/Ostiense Nightlife

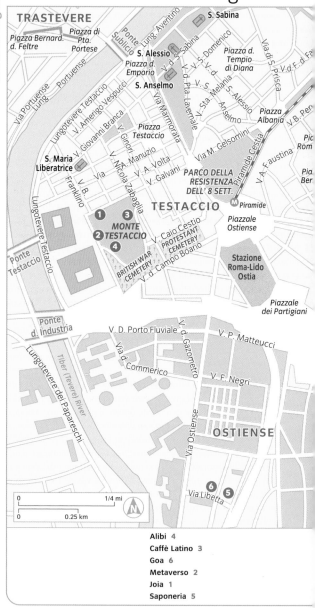

TRASTEVERE

Piazza Bernard. d. Feltre
Piazza di Pta. Portese
Ponte Sublicio
Lung. Aventino
S. Sabina
S. Alessio
Piazza d. Emporio
V. d. S. Sabina
V.-S. Domenico
Piazza d. Tempio di Diana
Via di S. Prisca
V.-S. V. d.
V.-S.-Melania-S. Alessio
S. Anselmo
Via Portuense
Lung. Portuense
Lungotevere Testaccio
V. Amerigo Vespucci
V. Giovanni Branca
Via Marmorata
Via d. Pta. Lavernale
V.-Sta.-Melania
Piazza Albania
V. B. Per
S. Maria Liberatrice
V. Gintri
V. Nicola Zabaglia
Piazza Testaccio
V. A. Manuzio
V. A. Volta
V. Galvani
Via M. Gelsomini
Pic Rom
V.-A.-F.austina
Pia Ber
Via B. Franklino
TESTACCIO
PARCO DELLA RESISTENZA DELL' 8 SETT.
Piramide Cestia
M Piramide
Lungotevere Testaccio
1 **3**
2 MONTE TESTACCIO
4
V. Caio Cestio
PROTESTANT CEMETERY
Piazzale Ostiense
Ponte Testaccio
BRITISH WAR CEMETERY
V. d. Campo Boario
Stazione Roma-Lido Ostia
Ponte d. Industria
Lungotevere dei Papareschi
Tiber (Tevere) River
V. D. Porto Fluviale
Via d. Commerico
V. d. Gazometro
V. P. Matteucci
V. F. Negri
Via Ostiense
Piazzale dei Partigiani
OSTIENSE
0 — 1/4 mi
0 — 0.25 km
6 **5**
Via Libetta

Alibi 4
Caffè Latino 3
Goa 6
Metaverso 2
Joia 1
Saponeria 5

Bars & Lounges

★★ Al Vino Al Vino MONTI
Cozy and convivial, this excellent
wine bar feels like the neighborhood's living room. Great selection
of antipasti, meats, and cheeses,
too. *Via dei Serpenti 19 (near Via
Panisperna).* ☎ *06-485803. Metro:
Cavour. Bus: 75. Map p 118.*

★★ Antico Caffè della Pace
PIAZZA NAVONA   Known as "Bar
della Pace," this boîte on a picturesque side street is the classic *centro storico* spot for people-watching.
Every night it's an entertaining mix
of fashionable Romans and the
tourists who come to gawk at them.
Via della Pace 5 (off Via di Parione).
☎ *06-6861216. Bus: 30, 70, 87, 492,
628. Map p 117.*

★★ Bartaruga JEWISH GHETTO   A
dark room with sagging armchairs
and bright frescoes, sassy bar staff,
and stiff drinks. The scene is arty and
intellectual but unpretentious—the
polar opposite of Rome's trendier
bars and lounges. *Piazza Mattei 9.*
☎ *06-6892299. Bus: 23, 271, or 280.
Tram: 8. Map p 117.*

★★ Casina Valadier SPANISH
STEPS/VILLA BORGHESE   In the
leafy grounds of the restaurant of
the same name, this is an exceed-
ingly romantic spot for a drink any

time of day. It's not the hippest
place in town, but with its comfy
canvas sofas and view over the *centro storico*, I'll overlook the fact that
Rod Stewart's standards are on
heavy rotation on the garden sound
system. *Piazza Bucarest (Viale del
Belvedere, Villa Borghese).* ☎ *06-
69922090. Metro: Spagna. Bus: 63,
116, 490, or 495. Map p 117.*

★ Dom Champagneria MONTI
Bubbly and beautiful people are the
main event at this sexy new addition
to Monti's burgeoning nightlife
scene. The dark, modern interior
features arty books velcroed to the
walls. Good *aperitivo* buffet. *Via
degli Zingari 49 (near Via dei Serpenti).* ☎ *06-45426401. Metro:
Cavour. Bus: 75. Map p 118.*

★★ Freni e Frizioni TRASTEVERE
"Brakes and Clutches" is a former
mechanics-garage-turned-nighttime-
hotspot, with an ethnic-inflected
aperitivo spread (think curried
risotto). On the adjacent square, an
effervescent crowd lounges against
stone walls and parked *motorini*.
*Via del Politeama 4–6 (near Piazza
Trilussa).* ☎ *06-58334210. Bus: 23,
271, or 280. Map p 117.*

★★ Le Coppelle 52 PANTHEON
Occupying most of a wonderfully
secluded piazza, this lounge catches

Roma di Notte: The city all lit up for the evening.

An evening of eating and drinking in Trastevere.

all the evening traffic coming or going to the hip restaurants in the vicinity. On balmy nights, the outdoor tables are highly prized real estate. *Piazza delle Coppelle 52 (off Via delle Coppelle).* ☎ *06-6832410. Bus: 30, 40, 62, 64, 70, 87, 492, or 571. Map p 117.*

★★ **Salotto 42** PANTHEON Jetsetters and wannabes congregate at this uber-hip "book bar," opened by a pair of Swedish and Roman models in 2004. Furnishings have a worn-in bohemian feel, inviting

hours of conversation, and there's a Scandinavian smorgasbord for Sunday brunch. *Piazza di Pietra 42 (off Via del Corso).* ☎ *06-6785804. Bus: 30, 40, 62, 64, 70, 87, 116, 492, or 571. Map p 117.*

★★ **Société Lutèce** PIAZZA NAVONA One of the first bars to introduce the Northern Italian *aperitivo* phenomenon to Rome, this stylish, laid-back spot is great for drinking and snacking before, after, or instead of dinner. *Piazza Montevecchio 17 (off Via dei Coronari).* ☎ *06-68301472. Bus: 30, 70, 87, 492, 628. Map p 117.*

★★ **Taverna del Campo** CAMPO DE' FIORI Roman hipsters ebb and flow through its outdoor tables from the *aperitivo* hour (6–7pm) till closing (2am), leaving peanut shells in their wake. *Campo de' Fiori 16 (at Via Baullari).* ☎ *06-6874402. Bus: 30, 40, 62, 64, 70, 87, 116, or 492. Tram: 8. Map p 117.*

★★ **Vineria Reggio** CAMPO DE' FIORI Night after night, this supercheap, social Campo drinking spot perpetuates *la dolce vita.* *Campo de' Fiori 15 (at Via Baullari).* ☎ *06-68803268. Bus: 30, 40, 62, 64, 70, 87, 116, or 492. Tram: 8. Map p 117.*

The Clubs of Monte Testaccio

Want to sample Rome's club scene but not sure where to start? **Monte Testaccio,** ancient Rome's pottery dump, is ringed with discos and lounges for all tastes, ages, and noise levels. Simply head for the three streets (Via Galvani, Via di Monte Testaccio, and Via Zabaglia) skirting the artificial mountain, and see what looks good to you. A few of my favorite standbys are **Metaverso** (Via di Monte Testaccio 38A; ☎ 06-5744712), **Joia** (Via Galvani 20; ☎ 06-5740802), and **Caffè Latino** (Via di Monte Testaccio 96; ☎ 06-57288556). Check the weekly listings mag *Roma C'è* to see what's on where. For all Testaccio clubs, take the Metro to Piramide, or bus 23, 30, 75, 95, 170, or 280, or tram 3. After midnight, take bus N3, N9, N10, or N11.

The Alexanderplatz Jazz Club.

Discos & Clubs

★★ Goa OSTIENSE   Consistently one of the best clubs in Rome, with an ethnic look, international DJs, and a *bella gente* crowd that's not too young, especially on weeknights. *Via Libetta 13 (off Via Ostiense).* ☎ *06-5748277. 20€ cover. Metro: Garbatella. Bus: 23, 271, or 280. Map p 120.*

★ Piper NORTHERN SUBURBS There's a winking, strutting, disco vibe at this historic venue. The multilevel dance floors make for good scoping of potential mates. Saturday nights are gay. *Via Tagliamento 9.* ☎ *06-8414459. 20€ cover. Bus: 63. Map p 118.*

★ Saponeria OSTIENSE   At this soap-factory-turned-dance-factory, the crowd tends to be squeaky clean and very good-looking—think Italian water polo players in Façonnable shirts and their female groupies. *Via degli Argonauti 20 (at Via Ostiense).* ☎ *06-5746999. 15€–20€ cover. Metro: Garbatella. Bus: 23, 271, or 280. Map p 120.*

Gay & Lesbian

★★ Alibi TESTACCIO   This consistently good gay disco, with an infamously heavy pickup scene, features music in a happy mix of house and techno. In summer, the dancing spills out to the club's fabulous rooftop. *Via di Monte Testaccio 40–47 (at Via Galvani).* ☎ *06-5743448. Metro: Piramide. Bus: 23, 30, 75, 95, 170, or 280. 12€–15€ cover (Fri–Sat only). Map p 120.*

★ Gender SAN GIOVANNI   An intimate, erotic lesbian/gay/transsexual club with strip shows and private cabins—equal opportunity for exhibitionists and voyeurs alike. *Via Faleria 9 (at Via Appia Nuova).* ☎ *06-70497638. 10€–15€ cover. Metro: San Giovanni or Re di Roma. Map p 118.*

Live Music

★ Alexanderplatz Jazz Club VATICAN   Smooth and classy, this low-ceilinged jazz joint is one of the best in Italy. In summer, the club sponsors the super-fab jazz festival at Villa Celimontana. *Via Ostia 9 (at Via Leone IV).* ☎ *06-39742171. 8€ cover. Metro: Ottaviano. Map p 118.*

★★ Big Mama TRASTEVERE With a reassuring reek of beer, this subterranean blues club is the closest thing in Rome to a honky-tonk. Top-notch blues, rock, and soul acts guarantee a good time, so the small, sticky wooden tables go fast. *Vicolo di Francesco a Ripa 18 (at Via San Francesco a Ripa).* ☎ *06-5812551. Cover 8€–12€. Bus: 23, 271, 280, 780, or H. Tram: 3 or 8. Map p 118.*

Oh, Those Roman Summer Nights

Every summer, the city does an epic job of erecting outdoor venues—part of a calendar of cultural events known as *Estate Romana*—where its citizens can party from June to September. In the *centro,* check out live music and bars at **Portal,** the swimming pool/sun deck on the river bank below Castel Sant'Angelo; or **Isola del Cinema,** the film festival on Tiber Island. In the fascist-era suburb of EUR to the south, **La Terrazza dell'Eur** is a nightclub on the roof of an official building, and there's a **Gay Village** entertainment complex set up off EUR's man-made lake. *Estate Romana's* offerings also go high-brow, with concerts and literature readings among the ruins. See www.estateromana.comune.roma.it.

★ **Fonclea** VATICAN This multi-room, English-style venue has a mellow happy hour and live sets of soul, funk, jazz, and rock. Pub food is served. *Via Crescenzio 82A (at Piazza Risorgimento).* ☎ *06-6896302. 10€ food/drink minimum. Metro: Ottaviano. Bus: 23, 81, 271, or 492. Tram: 19. Map p 118.*

Pubs

★ **Camden Town** ANCIENT ROME Owners Alberto and Carlo welcome a loyal young crowd nightly for pints and sporting events. Friendly English-speaking staff and a lively scene at the bar and tables prevail. *Via Ostilia 30A (at Via Capo d'Africa).* ☎ *06-7096322. Metro: Colosseo. Bus: 75, 81, 175. Tram: 3. Map p 118.*

★★ **Cork's Inn** PIAZZA VENEZIA/ MONTI   Veteran Roman pub manager Vincenzo opened this secluded indoor/outdoor joint in 2007, and it's been a huge hit with locals and English-speaking visitors ever since. All major sports are shown, but it's first and foremost a rugby bar. A great place to while away a mild evening, wearing jeans and flip-flops. *Via delle Tre Cannelle 8 (off Via Nazionale).* ☎ *06-6990986. Bus: 40, 64, or 70. Map p 117.*

★ **Fiddler's Elbow** TERMINI/MONTI The oldest Irish pub in Rome—always packed with a talkative crowd of locals, resident expats, travelers, and the odd priest. *Via dell'Olmata 43 (at Piazza Santa Maria Maggiore).* ☎ *06-4872110. Metro: Cavour or Termini. Bus: 70 or 75. Map p 118.* ●

Fiddler's Elbow, a popular Irish pub near the train station.

Arts & Entertainment Best Bets

Best **Entertainment, Period**
★★★ AS Roma or ★★ SS Lazio,
Stadio Olimpico (p 131)

Best **Classical Music**
★★ Accademia di Santa Cecilia,
*Largo Luciano Berio 3 Auditorium
(p 129)*

Best **Summer Festival**
★★ Villa Celimontana Jazz Festival, *Villa Celimontana (p 130)*

Best for **Living La Dolce Vita**
★★★ Baths of Caracalla, *Viale
delle Terme di Caracalla (p 130)*

Best **Excuse to Get Dressed Up**
★ Teatro dell'Opera, *Via Firenze 72
(p 129)*

Best **Place to Catch a Big-Bud-
get American Action Flick in
English or Italian**
★ Warner Village—Moderno,
Piazza della Repubblica 45 (p 131)

Best **Mellow Outdoor
Concerts**
★★ Villa Giulia, *Piazza di Villa Giulia
(p 130)*

Best **Crosstown Rivalry**
★★★ Roma-Lazio derby games,
*Foro Italico/Viale dello Stadio
Olimpico (p 132)*

Best **Athletics Complex**
★ Foro Italico, *Viale del Foro Italico/
Viale dei Gladiatori (p 131)*

Classical concerts are held in the nymphaeum, pictured here, at the Villa Giulia.

Previous page: Children playing outside the Colosseum

Centro Storico A&E

Alcazar 5
AS Roma store 2
Baths of Caracalla 8
Cinecittà 7

Metropolitan 1
Teatro dell'Opera 4
Villa Celimontana Festival Jazz 6
Warner Village–Moderno 3

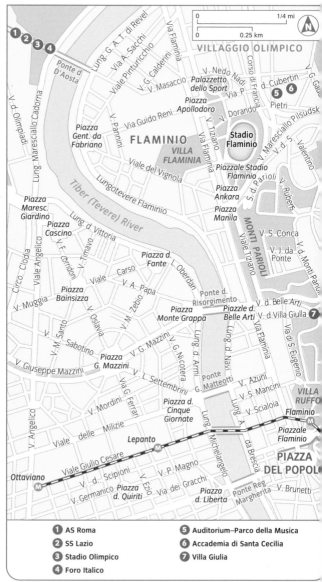

1 AS Roma
2 SS Lazio
3 Stadio Olimpico
4 Foro Italico
5 Auditorium–Parco della Musica
6 Accademia di Santa Cecilia
7 Villa Giulia

Classical Music

★★ Accademia di Santa Cecilia NORTHERN SUBURBS

Rome's premier symphony orchestra, founded by Palestrina in the 16th century, performs in the brand-new concert halls at the Auditorium–Parco della Musica. *Largo Luciano Berio 3 (Auditorium).* ☎ 06-80242501 (info) or 06-8082058 (tickets). www.santacecilia.it. Tickets 20€–100€. *Bus: 53, 217, 910, or M. Tram: 2. Map p 128.*

★★ Auditorium–Parco della Musica NORTHERN SUBURBS

This exciting multipurpose center for the arts, designed by Renzo Piano, brings a refreshing breath of modernity to Rome. Some say the three lead-roofed concert halls look like giant beetles, but the architecture is undeniably dramatic and the acoustics outstanding. The schedule features lots of folk singer–songwriter acts as well as traditional orchestras. Great cafes are on site, too. *Viale Pietro di Coubertin (Corso Francia/Viale Tiziano).* ☎ 199-109-783 (toll-free in Italy) or 06-3700106

Posters of upcoming arts attractions are everywhere in Rome, like this one advertising a musical play, Vampiri!

(from outside Italy). www.auditorium.com. Ticket prices vary. Bus: 53, 217, 910, or M. Tram: 2. Map p 128.

★ Teatro dell'Opera TERMINI

Performances tend to be good, but seldom great, at the financially troubled city opera. Still, the theater's ornate 19th-century interior is a perfect setting for a sophisticated

The Auditorium–Parca della Musica is a multipurpose center for the arts.

Music is everywhere in Rome, from symphony halls to the street, where guitarists like this one offer impromptu entertainment.

Roman night out. Recent productions have included *Carmen, La Fanciulla del West,* and such ballets as *Il Lago dei Cigni (Swan Lake)* and *Lo Schiaccianoci (The Nutcracker).* *Via Firenze 72 (at Via del Viminale).* ☎ *06-481601. www.operaroma.it. Tickets 115€–150€. Map p 127.*

Summer Venues

★★★ **Baths of Caracalla** AVENTINE   Attend a production of *Aïda* here, amid the towering ruins of the 3rd-century-A.D. caldarium, and you'll know the meaning of *la dolce vita.*

Viale delle Terme di Caracalla. July–Aug only. www.operaroma.it. Ticket prices vary. Metro: Circo Massimo. Bus: 30, 118, or 628. Map p 127.

★ **Tempietto** MULTIPLE LOCATIONS With outdoor classical concerts at the Theater of Marcellus and Villa Torlonia, or inside the Teatro Ghione, the Tempietto music series is an informal way to soak up some great atmosphere and culture. ☎ *06-87131590. www.tempietto.it. Tickets 18€.*

★★ **Villa Celimontana Festival Jazz** ANCIENT ROME   In this gorgeous 16th-cenurty park, a summer-long festival offers nightly jazz, blues, and rock acts, as well as temporary, miniature versions of some of Rome's top restaurants. *Piazza della Navicella (at Via Claudia).* ☎ *06-5897807. For table bookings,* ☎ *06-77073799. www.villacelimontanajazz. com. Tickets around 20€. Metro: Colosseo. Bus: 60, 75, 81, 87, 175, or 271. Tram: 3. Map p 127.*

★★ **Villa Giulia** VILLA BORGHESE It doesn't get much lovelier than an intimate classical concert here, in the nymphaeum (ornamental grotto built as a shrine to water nymphs) of a 16th-century villa. *Piazza di Villa Giulia (at Viale delle Belle Arti).* ☎ *06-39734576. Ticket prices vary. Tram: 3 or 19. Map p 128.*

Rome Performs

The performing arts do exist in Rome, but they've never been the city's highest priority. Having said that, the symphony is excellent, and summer sees an explosion of cultural offerings, with romantic concerts among ruins, operas in church courtyards, and jazz in the parks. The best tickets in town, however, are to soccer games at the Stadio Olimpico. For the most detailed information about what's on, the weekly listings mag *Roma C'è* (1.20€ at newsstands) is an indispensable resource. Tickets for most events can be bought online at www.listicket.it.

The Baron von Munchhausen set at the old Cinecittà film lots.

Cinemas

Alcazar TRASTEVERE   Single-screen cinema with films in *Versione Originale* on Monday. *Via Cardinale Merry del Val 14 (at Viale Trastevere).* ☎ *06-5880099. Tickets 7€. Bus: H or 780. Tram: 3 or 8. Map p 127.*

★ **Cinecittà** SOUTHERN SUBURBS Rome's legendary film lots had their heyday in the 1950s and '60s. Nowadays, more reality shows than silver-screen classics are shot here, but the sets from such epics as *Ben-Hur* are fascinating. Tours of the film lots are generally only available to students (free), arranged by calling the central line. **Note:** Cinecittà is developing a theme park to be called **Cinecittà World,** a 60-hectare (146-acre) park that will occupy a part of the current studios' premises. It promises to "transport visitors in the fanciest journeys of movie magic and entertainment." Stay tuned. *Via Tuscolana 1055.* ☎ *06-722931. Metro: Cinecittà. Map p 127.*

★ **Metropolitan** PIAZZA DEL POPOLO   This very central cinema usually has at least one screen showing films in *versione originale.* *Via del Corso 7* ☎ *06-32000933. Tickets 7€. Metro: Flaminio. Map p 127.*

★ **Warner Village—Moderno** TERMINI   One screen at this American-style multiplex is dedicated to films in *versione originale*—often something like *Saw IV. Piazza della* *Repubblica 45.* ☎ *06-47779111. Tickets 5.50€–7.50€. Metro: Repubblica. Bus: 40, 64, 70, or 170. Map p 127.*

Sports

★★★ **AS Roma** NORTHERN SUBURBS   La Roma wears yellow and red *(giallorosso),* draws fans from the city center and political left, and is Lazio's archrival. Team captain Francesco Totti is a local hero. See Stadio Olimpico, below. *Tickets can be purchased at the Stadio Olimpico on game day, at Lottomatica stores, or at the official Roma Store at Piazza Colonna 360.* ☎ *06-6786514. www.asroma.it. Tickets 20€–120€. Map p 128.*

★ **Foro Italico** NORTHERN SUBURBS   This sprawling athletics complex, dotted with umbrella pines and Fascist-era mosaics and statues, is home to soccer games, the Italian Open tennis tournament, and various other sporting events. *Viale del Foro Italico/Viale dei Gladiatori.* ☎ *06-36858218. Ticket prices vary by event. Bus: 32, 271, or 280. Tram: 225. Map p 128.*

★★ **SS Lazio** NORTHERN SUBURBS   Rome's other *Serie A* soccer team wears light blue and white *(biancoceleste);* its followers hail from the monied suburbs. See Stadio Olimpico, below. *Tickets can be purchased at the Stadio Olimpico on game day, at Lottomatica stores, or at the Lazio*

GOOOOOOL! Soccer, Rome-Style

To experience Roman culture at its most fervent, don't go to Mass—go to a soccer game. Full of pageantry, dramatic tension, and raw emotion, the home games of **Roma** and **Lazio,** the city's two *Serie A* (Italian premier league) teams, can be far more spectacular than any fancy theater event, and certainly more interactive (when was the last time you got beaned in the head by a sandwich, thrown by an irate fan, at *La Bohème?*). *Romanisti* far outnumber *Laziali*, but both fan bases pack the Stadio Olimpico, coloring the stands with the red and yellow of Roma or the light blue and white of Lazio, every weekend from September to June. If you go to a game, invest in a team scarf (sold at concession stands outside the stadium), and learn a few stadium choruses—both teams have a few easy ones set to the tune of "The Entertainer" and the march from *Aïda*. To score huge points with the locals, stop by Porta Portese (see chapter 4) before the game and pick up some colored smoke bombs *(fumogeni)* or firecrackers *(petardi)* to set off outside the stadium—true tailgating, Italian-style! Buy game tickets at *tabacchi* stores bearing the Lottomatica logo.

Point on Via Farini 34, ☎ *06-4826768. www.sslazio.it. Tickets 20€–120€. Map p 128.*

★★ **Stadio Olimpico** NORTHERN SUBURBS   For better or for worse, there is no better place to soak up modern Roman culture than at the soccer stadium. The Olimpico,

Ludovic Giuly of AS Roma.

Rome's 73,000-capacity venue, is where the AS Roma and SS Lazio *Serie A* (premier league) teams play at least once a week from September to June. *Foro Italico/Viale dello Stadio Olimpico.* ☎ *06-3237333 (box office). Tickets 20€–120€. Bus: 32, 271, or 280. Tram: 225. Map p 128.* ●

Lodging Best Bets

The handsome facade of the Aldrovandi Palace hotel.

Best **"Only in Rome" Hideaway**
★★★ The Inn at the Roman Forum $$$$ *Via degli Ibernesi 30 (p 143)*

Best **Stylish Retreat**
★★★ Villa Laetitia $$$ *Lungotevere delle Armi 22–23 (p 146)*

Best **Cheap & Centrally Located Accommodations**
★ Sole al Biscione $ *Via del Biscione 76 (p 146);* and ★ Ivanhoe $ *Via dei Ciancaleoni 50 (p 143)*

Best **for Hobnobbing with Hotshots**
★★★ Hotel de Russie $$$$ *Via del Babuino 9 (p 142);* and ★★★ Portrait Suites $$$$ *Via Bocca di Leone 23 (p 145)*

Best **Vacation-Rental Agency**
★★ Roman Reference $–$$$ *(p 141)*

Best **for Families**
★ Aldrovandi Palace $$$ *Via Ulisse Aldrovandi 15 (p 140);* and ★ Lancelot $$ *Via Capo d'Africa 47 (p 143)*

Best **Gem in an Overpriced Area**
★★ Modigliani $$–$$$ *Via della Purificazione 42 (p 144)*

Best **in an Authentic Roman Neighborhood**
★★ Santa Maria $$ *Vicolo del Piede 2 (p 145);* and ★ Arco del Lauro B&B $ *Via dell'Arco de' Tolomei 27–29 (p 140)*

Best **Escape from Vespa Drone**
★★ Aventino Hotels $$–$$$ *Via S. Melania 19 (p 140)*

Best **for Artists & Poets**
★ Locarno $$–$$$ *Via della Penna 22 (p 143)*

Best **for Visiting Cardinals**
★ Columbus $$–$$$ *Via della Conciliazione 33 (p 141)*

Best **Cheap Sleep (Minus the Bed Bugs)**
★ Colors $ *Via Boezio 31 (p 141)*

Previous page: A studio room at Hotel de Russie.

Centro Storico Lodging

| 0 | | 1/8 mile |
| 0 | 100 meters | |

- V. d. Coronari
- V. d. Montevecchio
- S. Maria d. Pace
- Piazza Cinque Luna
- Piazza Capranica
- **PIAZZA NAVONA**
- Corso del Rinascimento
- V. d. Salvatore
- V. Giustiniani
- Piazza d. Rotonda
- V. d. Pace
- V. S. Maria d. Anima
- V. d. Vecchia
- V. d. Seminario
- **Pantheon**
- **S. Maria Sopra Minerva**
- V. d. Corallo
- V. d. Gov. Vecchio
- V. d. Parione
- Piazza d. Chiesa Nuova
- V. Sora
- Piazza Pasquino
- V. Teatro Valle
- V. Monterone
- V. d. S. Chiara
- Piazza di Minerva
- V. d. Gesù
- V. dei Pellegrino
- Corso Vittorio Emanuele II
- **S. Andrea della Valle**
- V. d. Torre Argentina
- Largo d. Torre Argentina
- Piazza d. Gesù
- V. Cappellari
- V. Monserrato
- V. d. Baullari
- V. d. Chiavari
- **PIAZZA CAMPO D. FIORI**
- Piazza Farnese
- V. d. Giubbonari
- V. d. Arco d. Monte
- V. d. Specchi
- V. d. Chiodaroli
- Largo Arenula
- Via Giulia
- L. d. Tebaldi
- **S. Salvatore in Onda**
- V. d. Pettinari
- Via d. Zoccolette
- V. Arenula
- Via Portico
- V. d. Catalana
- **Teatro di Marcello**
- Ponte Sisto
- Lungotevere dei Vallati
- Tiber (Tevere) River
- Lungotevere dei Cenci
- Piazza Trilussa
- Lung. Raffaello Sanzio
- Ponte Garibaldi
- **ISOLA TIBERINA (TIBER ISLAND)**
- Ponte Fabricio
- Piazza d. Renzi
- V. d. Moro
- V. d. Renella
- Piazza G.G. Belli
- Lung. d. Anguillara
- Ponte Cestio
- **San Bartolomeo**
- Piazza S. Maria in Trastevere
- Via d. Lungaretta
- **TRASTEVERE**
- **S. Maria in Trastevere**
- Piazza S. Sonnino
- V. d. Salumi
- Piazza in Piscinula
- Ponte Palatino

1, 2, 3, 4, 5, 6, 7, 8 (map markers)

Arco del Lauro B&B 8	Residenza Santa Maria 7
Della Lunetta 3	Santa Maria 6
Mimosa 1	Smeraldo 5
Pomezia 2	Sole al Biscione 4

Rome Lodging

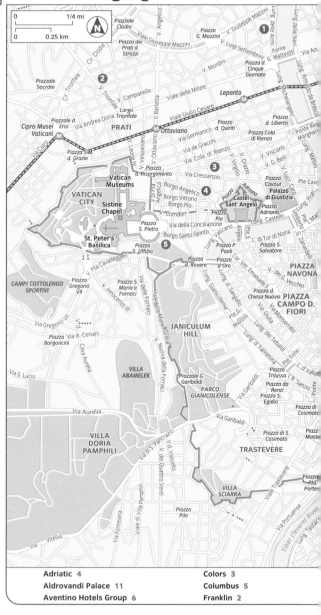

Adriatic 4	**Colors 3**
Aldrovandi Palace 11	**Columbus 5**
Aventino Hotels Group 6	**Franklin 2**

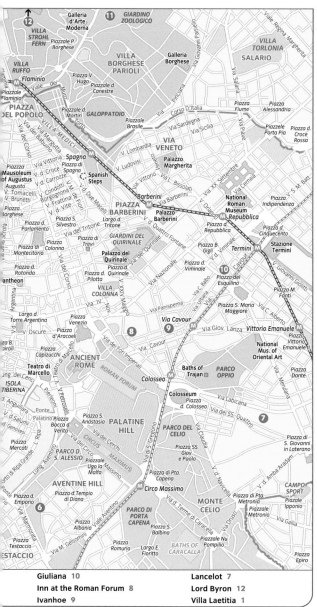

Giuliana **10**

Inn at the Roman Forum **8**

Ivanhoe **9**

Lancelot **7**

Lord Byron **12**

Villa Laetitia **1**

Tridente & Campo Marzio Lodging

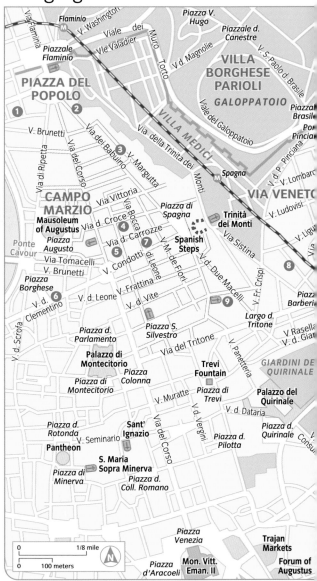

Casa Howard **9**	Hotel De Russie **2**	Modigliani **8**
Fontanella Borghese **6**	La Lumière **5**	Panda **4**
Forte **3**	Locarno **1**	Portrait Suites **7**

Rome Hotels A to Z

★ **Adriatic** VATICAN Within easy walking distance of the *centro storico*, Castel Sant'Angelo, and St. Peter's, the simple but spacious rooms here are perfect for budget-conscious travelers who want a convenient location but not a lot of amenities. A partly covered common terrace is great for sunning, reading, or sipping wine with fellow travelers. *Via Vitelleschi 25.* ☎ *06-68808080. www.adriatichotel.com. 42 units. Doubles 90€–130€. AE, MC, V. Bus: 23, 40, 271, or 280. Map p 136.*

★ **Aldrovandi Palace** VILLA BORGHESE Occupying some seriously prize real estate in the gorgeous greenery north of Villa Borghese, this classy hotel boasts a swimming pool and all modern amenities. *Via Ulisse Aldrovandi 15.* ☎ *06-3223993. www.aldrovandi. com. 135 units. Doubles 250€–500€. AE, MC, V. Bus: 52 or 53. Tram: 3 or 19. Map p 136.*

★ **Arco del Lauro B&B** TRASTE-VERE Vivacious Lorenza is your hostess at this clean and modern B&B on the quiet side of Trastevere, just across the river from Tiber Island and the Jewish Ghetto. Breakfast is served at a typical Roman bar on a nearby piazza. *Via dell'Arco de Tolomei 27–29.* ☎ *06-97840350 or 346-2443212. www.arcodellauro.it. 6 units. Doubles 95€–135€. No credit cards. Bus: 23, 271, or 280. Map p 135.*

★★ **Aventino Hotels Group** AVENTINE Of these three converted villas on the leafy and prestigious Aventine Hill, the San Anselmo is the chicest and most luxurious, the Aventino has cheerful 1930s appeal, and the Villa San Pio is like visiting your long-lost, old-money Roman relatives. All are blessedly tranquil. *Via S. Melania 19.* ☎ *06-5745231. www.aventinohotels.com. 100 units (in the Aventino Hotels Group). Doubles 230€–400€. AE, MC, V. Metro: Circo Massimo. Bus: 95 or 175. Tram: 3. Map p 136.*

★★ **Casa Howard** SPANISH STEPS This stylish, intimate guest-house features luxe fabrics like Toile

The stylish Casa Howard.

The rooms are stylish and comfortable at Forte.

de Jouy and Shanghai silk, fresh flowers in every unique room, and a Turkish bath. Such luxury, at these prices, is unheard of in Rome. *Via Capo le Case 18 and Via Sistina 149.* ☎ *06-69924555. www.casahoward. com. 10 units. Doubles 170€–250€. AE, MC, V. Metro: Spagna. Map p 138.*

★ **Colors** VATICAN Perfect for budget travelers in search of company, this friendly, colorful inn offers private and hostel-style rooms, as well as a kitchen and washing machine. *Via Boezio 31.* ☎ *06-6874030. www.colorshotel.com.*

15 units. Dorms from 15€, doubles 50€–120€. No credit cards. Metro: Ottaviano. Bus: 23 or 492. Map p 136.

★ **Columbus** VATICAN This upscale inn, a stone's throw from St. Peter's, was once home to a long line of popes and cardinals. Many of the somber-toned rooms preserve their original 16th-century wood ceilings and stucco work. *Via della Conciliazione 33.* ☎ *06-6865435. www.hotelcolumbus.net. 92 units. Doubles 175€–350€. AE, DC, MC, V. Bus: 30, 40, or 64. Map p 136.*

Vacation Rentals (Short-Term Apartments)

Rome is among the growing number of cities where renting an apartment is often more attractive than staying in a hotel—especially for folks trying to stretch the U.S. dollar. In an apartment, you'll live like a Roman, and almost certainly save money, since nightly rates are usually lower than those of hotel rooms. And you'll be able to shop for food at the local markets and cook for yourself instead of going out to pricey meals. Located throughout the city, Rome's vacation rentals come in all sizes and price ranges, though amenities (satellite TV, washer/dryer, air-conditioner) vary from property to property. Most have a minimum-stay requirement of 3 nights. ★★ **Roman Reference** (☎ 06-48903612; www.romanreference.com) is a responsive and helpful agency with a large database of apartments in great locations.

A Note on the Grande Dames

Among Rome's well-known five-star hotels, there is no one "right" address, and they're all so astronomically expensive these days—especially owing to the weak U.S. dollar—that I've chosen to primarily review lesser-known, less-pricey, and more-interesting lodging options. For the record, the most-prestigious big hotels in Rome are the Eden, the Excelsior, the Hassler, the Hotel de Russie (reviewed below), and the St. Regis.

Della Lunetta CAMPO DE' FIORI Spartan accommodations in a prime location, though light sleepers might want to stay away. *Piazza del Paradiso 68.* ☎ *06-6875929. 40 units. Doubles 90€–150€. MC, V. Bus: 40, 62, 64, 70, 87, 492, or 571. Map p 135.*

★ **Fontanella Borghese** PANTHEON   Occupying two floors of a palazzo that once belonged to the Borghese family, this is a noble address (equidistant from the Pantheon, Spanish Steps, and Piazza del Popolo) at sort-of plebeian prices. It's not a fancy place, but the classically decorated, family-friendly rooms are bright and spacious. *Largo Fontanella Borghese 84.* ☎ *06-68809504. www.fontanella borghese.com. 29 units. Doubles 150€–210€. AE, MC, V. Bus: 70, 81, 87, 116, 492. Map p 138.*

★ **Forte** SPANISH STEPS   The location, on one of Rome's loveliest streets, can't be beat. The small-ish rooms are comfortable and (mostly) contemporary, and the prices are certainly low for this part of town. *Via Margutta 61.* ☎ *06-3207625. www.hotelforte.com. 21 units. Doubles 156€–256€. AE, MC, V. Metro: Spagna. Map p 139.*

★★ **Franklin** VATICAN   Book a Pop, Rock, or Blues double at this music-themed, refreshingly modern boutique hotel a short walk north of the Vatican. Amenity-filled rooms feature canopy beds, satellite TV, free Wi-Fi, travertine bathrooms (some with disco ball!), and Bang & Olufsen stereos. All guests can make use of the hotel's 400-CD library. Special rooms available for families with small children. *Via Rodi 29.* ☎ *06-3903165. www.franklin hotelrome.it. 22 units. Doubles 100€–490€. AE, MC, V. Metro: Ottaviano or Cipro-Musei Vaticani. Bus: 23. Map p 136.*

Giuliana TERMINI   The Santacroce family and their staff will bend over backwards to make you feel welcome at this moderate inn near the train station and Santa Maria Maggiore. Simple but comfy rooms are done up in crimson and buttercream, and the bathrooms are surprisingly large. *Via Depretis 70.* ☎ *06-4880795. www.hotelgiuliana. com. 11 units. Doubles 90€–180€. AE, MC, V. Metro: Cavour. Bus: 70 or 75. Map p 136.*

★★ **Hotel de Russie** PIAZZA DEL POPOLO   It has the best location of Rome's five-star hotels, a clean neoclassical look, and tons of high-profile guests. The hotel's U-shape encloses a fabulous terraced garden, with bars, restaurants, and grottos sweeping up toward the Pincio. *Via del Babuino 9.* ☎ *06-328881. www. hotelderussie.it. 125 units. Doubles* from 450€. AE, DC, MC, V. Metro: Flaminio. Map p 138.

★★★ Inn at the Roman Forum

MONTI Only in Rome—this new boutique inn on a silent side street is one of most wonderful properties I've seen in recent years. Rooms are tastefully luxurious, with ethnic silks, soothing tones, and spacious bathrooms. The fifth floor Master Garden Rooms (from 450€) have private patios surrounded by flowers and greenery, ochre walls, and busts of emperors! The hotel's roof lounge has views of the Campidoglio, and for archaeology buffs, there's an ancient Roman crypoporticus behind the lobby. *Via degli Ibernesi 30.* ☎ *06-69190970. www. theinnattheromanforum.com. 15 units. Doubles 210€–600€. AE, MC, V. Metro: Cavour. Bus: 75, 85, 87, 175, or 571. Map p 136.*

★ Ivanhoe ANCIENT ROME

The rooms are all private, though there's a hostel-like feel to this basic but friendly inn in the heart of the hip Monti neighborhood. A well-used common room off the lobby is great

The Art Deco lobby in the Lord Byron hotel.

for meeting fellow guests. Those willing to rough it a bit can save by booking rooms without private bath. *Via de' Ciancaleoni 50.* ☎ *06-486813. www.hotelivanhoe.it. 20 units. Doubles 80€–140€. AE, MC, V. Metro: Cavour. Bus: 75, 85, 87, 175, 571. Map p 136.*

★ La Lumière SPANISH STEPS

Country guesthouse feel in a cosmopolitan location. Spacious rooms feature soft blues and mauves and beautiful hardwood floors. *Via Belsiana 72.* ☎ *06-69380806. www.la lumieredipiazzadispagna.com. 10 units. Doubles 150€–500€. AE, MC, V. Metro: Spagna. Map p 138.*

★ Lancelot ANCIENT ROME

This friendly three-star with surprisingly large and bright doubles (and free Wi-Fi) attracts a veritable United Nations of return guests. Full- and half-board options are great for families on a budget, and kids can play at the nearby Villa Celimontana. *Via Capo d'Africa 47.* ☎ *06-70450615. www. lancelothotel.com. 60 units. Doubles 150€–254€. AE, MC, V. Metro: Colosseo. Bus: 60, 75, 87, 175, or 571. Map p 136.*

★ Locarno PIAZZA DEL POPOLO

Artistic types love this shabby peacock of a hotel: The Art Deco furnishings are worn in places, but a feeling of old-world elegance remains. Ask for a deluxe room in the eastern annex, as rooms in the main building are dowdy and a bit melancholy. *Via della Penna 22.* ☎ *06-3610841. www.hotellocarno. com. 66 units. Doubles 230€–320€. AE, MC, V. Metro: Flaminio. Map p 138.*

★★ Lord Byron PARIOLI

Bordering Villa Borghese, in Rome's most prestigious residential area, this elegant palazzo oozes Art Deco style. Guest rooms, done up in curved, lacquered wood and richly colored carpet, are romantic, sleek, and

A breakfast spread at Modigliani.

chic. Be sure to book a renovated room, as some floors have yet to be updated. The on-site restaurant, Sapori del Lord Byron, is outstanding. *Via Giuseppe de Notaris 5.* ☎ *06-3220404. www.lordbyron hotel.com. 34 units. Doubles 330€– 500€. AE, MC, V. Tram: 3, 19. Map p 136.*

Mimosa PANTHEON   This budget stalwart in the heart of the *centro*

storico enjoys great word of mouth, so book early. Decor is hodge-podge at best, but the rooms are bright, and there are larger units suitable for families with small children. Mention Frommer's for a 10% discount. *Via di Santa Chiara 61.* ☎ *06-68801753. www.hotelmimosa. net. 11 units. Doubles 77€–118€. MC, V. Bus: 40, 62, 64, 70, 87, 492, or 571. Map p 135.*

★★ Modigliani VIA VENETO   Cheerful Roman hospitality and fantastic value near the top of the Spanish Steps. Accommodations are clean and classic, and there's a big common area off the lobby. West-facing rooms on the 5th and 6th floors have heart-stopping views over the *centro* and St. Peter's. Owners Marco and Giulia are a delight—be sure to read their "newsletter." *Via della Purificazione 42.* ☎ *06-42815226. www.hotel modigliani.com. 23 units. Doubles 155€–197€. AE, MC, V. Metro: Barberini. Bus: 62, 95, 175, or 492. Map p 138.*

Panda SPANISH STEPS   On a cafe-filled street in the heart of Rome's pricey shopping district, the Panda

A typical room in the Panda pensione.

The fabulous roof terrace at Portrait Suites.

is a basic, pleasant choice, where a weeklong stay costs less than an Armani suit. *Via della Croce 35.* ☎ *06-6780179. www.hotelpanda.it. 20 units. Doubles 150€–350€. MC, V. Metro: Spagna. Map p 138.*

Pomezia CAMPO DE' FIORI   While it offers few frills, the Pomezia provides more coziness and harmony of decor than other Campo de' Fiori two-stars. *Via dei Chiavari 13.* ☎ *06-6861371. 25 units. Doubles 100€–150€. AE, MC, V. Bus: 40, 62, 64, 70, 87, 492, or 571. Map p 135.*

★★★ Portrait Suites SPANISH STEPS   Fashionistas with money to spare, look no further than this boutique guesthouse run by the Ferragamo-owned Lungarno hotel group. Swanky and uncluttered are the keywords here, but warmth and amusing Italian flair aren't lacking in the ultra-stylish room decor. The roof terrace, with its overstuffed cushions, romantic candlelight, and exclusive company, is the epitome of modern Roman fabulousness. Superb staff. *Via Bocca di Leone 23.* ☎ *06-69380742. www.lungarno hotels.com. 15 units. Suites from 700€. AE, MC, V. Metro: Spagna. Map p 138.*

★ Residenza Santa Maria TRASTEVERE   This spin-off of the Santa Maria (below) opened in 2007. It may lack the garden space of its older sister but makes up for it with more spacious, family-friendly rooms, high, exposed-wood-ceilings, ancient Roman artifacts uncovered during the restoration, and a warm staff. *Via dell'Arco di San Calisto 20.* ☎ *06-58335103. www.residenzasanta maria.com. 6 units. Doubles 175€–260€. AE, MC, V. Bus: 23, 271, or 280. Tram: 8. Map p 135.*

★★ Santa Maria TRASTEVERE   An amazing find in hotel-deprived Trastevere, the Santa Maria feels like a 16th-century motel, with simple chalet-style rooms and a pretty courtyard with orange trees. Comfy breakfast room/lounge/bar. *Vicolo del Piede 2.* ☎ *06-5894626. www. htlsantamaria.com. 19 units. Doubles 175€–260€. AE, MC, V. Bus: 23, 271, or 280. Tram: 8. Map p 135.*

★ Smeraldo CAMPO DE' FIORI Well-priced but cramped, this *centro storico* "emerald" has a few shining facets, including Internet access and air-conditioning in rooms, and a

The serene and sophisticated Villa Laetitia.

pretty roof garden. *Vicolo dei Chiodaroli 9.* ☎ *06-6875929. www. smeraldoroma.com. 50 units. Doubles 100€–160€. AE, MC, V. Bus: 40, 62, 64, 70, 87, 492, or 571. Map p 135.*

★ **Sole al Biscione** CAMPO DE' FIORI   Rooms are basic (and can be loud when school groups lodge here), but the multilevel courtyard garden, open to all guests, overflows with Roman charm. *Via del Biscione 76.* ☎ *06-68806873. www. solealbiscione.it. 60 units. Doubles 100€–160€. No credit cards. Bus: 40, 62, 64, 70, 87, 492, or 571. Map p 135.*

★★★ **Villa Laetitia** PRATI   Set in the lush and tranquil back garden of a 100-year-old villa, each lovely suite at Anna Fendi's first Roman-lodging venture is decorated with 19th- and 20th-century antiques and original pieces—by the likes of Picasso and Lagerfeld—collected by Mrs. Fendi herself. All rooms have kitchens, and all but one unit have outdoor living space. The central building is set to open in late 2008 with more guest rooms, an events space, and a state-of-the-art spa. *Lungotevere delle Armi 22–23.* ☎ *06-3226776. www.villalaetitia.com. 15 units. Doubles 150€–350€. AE, MC, V. Tram: 19. Map p 136.* ●

Tivoli: Hadrian's Villa

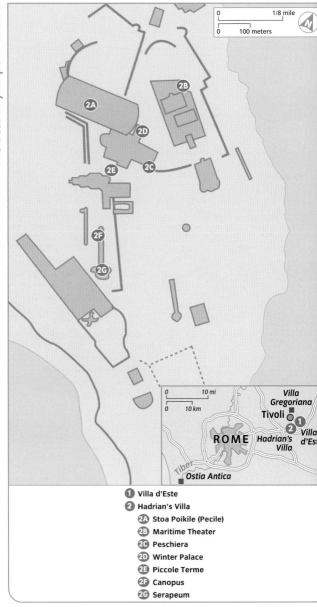

1 Villa d'Este
2 Hadrian's Villa
2A Stoa Poikile (Pecile)
2B Maritime Theater
2C Peschiera
2D Winter Palace
2E Piccole Terme
2F Canopus
2G Serapeum

Previous page: A mosaic at Hadrian's Villa.

The most classic Roman day trip, **Tivoli** lies about 32km (20 miles) west of the city and is home to the fountain-filled 16th-century Villa d'Este and the fantastically unique ancient ruins of Villa Adriana. Transportation to Tivoli can be slow; allow a full day.

1 ★★★ Villa d'Este. It's all about the fountains at this pleasure palace, commissioned in 1550 by Renaissance noble and cardinal Ippolito d'Este. Throughout the lush, steeply sloping gardens, whimsical grottoes, rushing flumes, reflecting pools, musical fountains, and bizarre gurgling "trees" delight and charm. ⏱ *45 min. Piazza Trento 1.* ☎ *0774-312070 or 199-766166 (toll-free from Italy). 6.50€. Tues–Sun 9am–6:15pm May–Sept; 8:30am–4pm Oct–Apr. From Rome: Cotral bus from Metro Ponte Mammolo, about 45 min. From Villa Adriana, regional bus to Tivoli, about 15 min.*

2 ★★★ Hadrian's Villa (Villa Adriana). Hadrian's sprawling estate (A.D. 118–34) was as much a summer retreat from the stifling air in Rome as it was a place where the emperor could fulfill all his architectural fantasies.

Near the entrance, the **★ Stoa Poikile** pool was once surrounded by a shady colonnade. The delightfully inventive **★★★ Maritime Theater** was where the emperor meditated and swam laps. The **★ Peschiera** was a giant aquarium, handy for seafood dinners this far inland. The attached **★ Winter Palace** has some of its heating system intact, as well as great views toward Rome. At the **★ Piccole Terme (Small Baths),** look for marvelous stuccoes on the ceiling vaults. The exquisite **★★★ Canopus,** a long pool with broken Assyrian arcades and statuary, terminates in the **★★ Serapeum,** a dining room whose front "wall" was a thin sheet of water, fed by the aqueduct above, that cooled the air. ⏱ *1½ hr. Villa Adriana (Tivoli).* ☎ *0774-382733. 6.50€. Daily 9am–6:30pm Apr–Sept; 9am–5pm Oct–Mar. From Rome: Cotral bus to Villa Adriana from Metro station Ponte Mammolo, about 45 min. From Villa d'Este (Tivoli town), regional bus to Villa Adriana, about 15 min.*

The statue-filled Canopus at Hadrian's Villa.

Ostia Antica

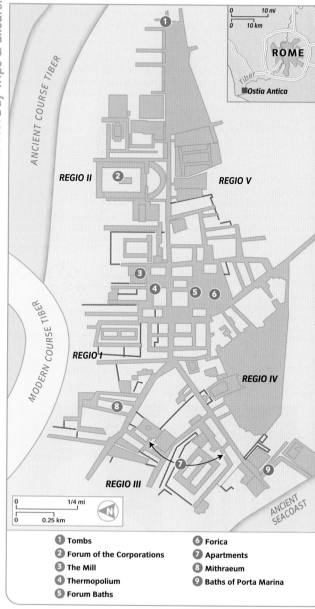

ANCIENT COURSE TIBER

ROME

Tiber

■ *Ostia Antica*

0 — 10 mi
0 — 10 km

REGIO II

❷

REGIO V

MODERN COURSE TIBER

❸

❹ ❺ ❻

REGIO I

REGIO IV

❽

❼

❾

REGIO III

ANCIENT SEACOAST

0 — 1/4 mi
0 — 0.25 km

Ⓝ

❶ Tombs
❷ Forum of the Corporations
❸ The Mill
❹ Thermopolium
❺ Forum Baths
❻ Forica
❼ Apartments
❽ Mithraeum
❾ Baths of Porta Marina

The port of ancient Rome lay where the Tiber flowed into the Mediterranean (**ostia** is "mouth" in Latin). The seacoast receded, and the river course changed, leaving ★★★ **Ostia Antica** landlocked and obsolete. Surrounded by trees and rarely crowded, the ruins are varied, extensive, and fun to explore, even better than Pompeii for understanding how the ancients used to live. The visit can easily be done in half a day, or combined with a trip to the beach at Ostia Lido (p 157) for a full day's excursion. Bring a picnic, or eat at the site's pleasant cafe.

1 **Tombs.** The road leading into the ancient town proper is lined with tombs; as was the custom throughout Rome, burials had to be outside the city walls.

2 ★★★ **Forum of the Corporations.** Farther into town, behind an ancient theater, is this wonderful former square where the shops of various importers have mosaics that indicate their cargo, from oil to elephants.

3 ★★ **The Mill.** Here, grinding stones and bread ovens are still in place.

4 ★★ **Thermopolium.** These hard-to-find ruins were once a stylish snack bar, serving hot and cold food and drinks.

5 ★ **Forum Baths.** Notice especially the pipes that heated the marble-clad walls of these baths.

6 ★★ **Forica.** This tour-group magnet was the public latrine, with neat rows of toilets still open to the sewer below (now neutral-smelling).

7 ★ **Apartments.** All over the site, modest-to-extravagant apartment clusters are open for wandering—be sure to visit the posh ★ **Garden Apartments,** the ★ **Insula of the Charioteers,** and the ★ **House of the Dioscuri.**

8 ★★ **Mithraeum.** This creepy chamber is found under the Baths of

A lovely mosaic at Ostia Antica.

Mithras and was where 2nd-century-A.D. initiates of the god of Mithras performed rituals.

9 ★★ **Baths of Porta Marina.** Check out the hilarious ancient mosaics of bodybuilders here.
🕐 *2–3 hr. Viale dei Romagnoli 117.* ☎ *06-56358099. 6.50€. Apr–Oct Tues–Sun 9am–6pm; Nov–Mar 8:30am–4pm. Train to Ostia Antica from Stazione Porta San Paolo (Metro: Piramide), about 30 min.*

Pompeii & Naples

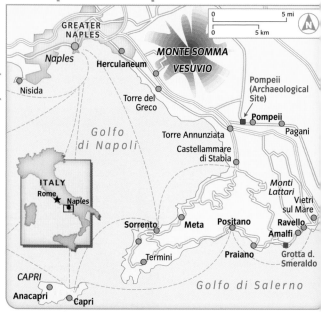

The ancient Roman town of Pompeii, buried by the devastating volcanic eruption of Mount Vesuvius in A.D. 79, is the most visited cultural site in Italy. At 3 hours away, Pompeii may not be the most convenient day trip from Rome, but it's worth the effort. For a real treat, stop in the city of Naples on the way back for a panoramic drive through Italy's most naturally stunning city.

Getting There

Take the train to Napoli Centrale station (about 2 hr.), then a Sorrento-bound *Circumvesuviana* (commuter train) to Pompei Scavi (about 30 min.). The *Circumvesuviana* also stops at Ercolano (the excavations of ancient Herculaneum).

★★★ **Scavi di Pompei.** Pompeii is a vast site—to see the best of it, you'll have to cover a lot of ground. Pick up a map at the entrance to get your bearings. While not everything is well preserved, what has survived will strike you as uncannily sophisticated and often luxurious. The **Forum** was the center of civic life in Pompeii, but not its most interesting attraction today (except for the plaster casts of bodies stored along the north side). To the east are the **Forum Baths,** with their elegant condensation-management system and locker-room cubbyholes. **House of the Vettii** is popular for its racy frescoes and preserved kitchen

The plaster cast of a man killed by the eruption of Mt. Vesuvius at Pompeii in 79 A.D.

implements. The fabulous **House of the Faun, House of Menander,** and **House of the Tragic Poet** are where the wealthiest Pompeiians lived. At the eastern end of the site (a 20-min. walk from the entrance) is the **Amphitheater,** with the gladiators' barracks adjacent. On your way back, be sure to see the **Lupanare** (the town brothel, with X-rated frescoes above each door), the charming and fantastically preserved **Small Theater,** and the **Stabian Baths,** which has great vaults and more plaster casts of crawling bodies caught in desperate attempts to survive. (Most deaths during the eruption were actually caused by asphyxiation from the volcano's toxic fumes.) **Villa of the Mysteries,** famous for its beautiful and enigmatic frescoes, is a good 10-minute walk north of the main part of the site. ⏱ *At least 3 hr. Entrance: Porta Marina.* ☎ *081-8575347. 11€. Daily 8:30am–5pm Nov–Mar; 8:30am–7:30pm Apr–Oct.*

★★★ **Naples.** Sadly, most people associate petty scams and organized crime with Napoli, but it's still safer than most big cities—and heart-stoppingly beautiful. Don't miss such knockout sights as **Piazza Plebiscito,** seaside **Chiaia** and **Via Partenope, Castel dell'Ovo,** the heights of **Vomero** and tony **Posillipo,** and **Palazzo Reale,** as well as such characteristic neighborhoods as **Spaccanapoli** and **Quartieri Spagnoli.**

Fat City

As the birthplace of pizza and Sophia Loren (in nearby Pozzuoli), bella Napoli is known for its bounty—even the main drag in Pompeii is called Via dell'Abbondanza (Street of Abundance). From Cape Misenum to Sorrento, the Bay of Naples is leaping with the best fish the Med has to offer. The fertile volcanic soil on the sunny slopes of Mt. Vesuvius is home to citrus groves that yield softball-size lemons. Thanks to a unique combination of sea air and local grass, Naples's region, Campania, is the only place in the world where real *mozzarella di bufala* can be produced. Make time for sipping fresh-squeezed lemonade, crunching into amazing fried calamari, or sinking your teeth into a fat slice of Neapolitan pizza with a huge hunk of melted mozzarella on top.

Castelli Romani

Lago di
Bracciano

Campagnano
di Roma

Anguillara

Monterotondo

Mentana

Villa Gregoriana

Tivoli

Villa Adriana
(Hadrian's Villa)

Villa
d'Este

ROME

Frascati ❶

Grottaferrata ❷

Marino

Castelgandolfo ❸

Rocca di
Papa

Albano ❻

❹ Nemi

Ariccia ❺

Genzano

Velletri

Tiber

Ostia Antica

Lido
di Ostia

Pomezia

Ardea

Aprilia

Tyrrhenian
Sea

Nettuno

Anzio

| 0 | 10 mi |
| 0 | 10 km |

❶ Frascati
❷ Grottaferrata
❸ Castelgandolfo
❹ Nemi
❺ Genzano
☕ Ariccia

The best way to see these charming "Roman castles" (hill towns) just south of the city is to rent a car (p 162). On the way, stop and see the spectacular ruins of Roman aqueducts at the Parco degli Acquedotti (heading south on Via Appia Nuova, turn left on Viale Appio Claudio). Alternatively, the Castelli Romani are served by COTRAL buses from the Anagnina Metro station. There's also a direct train from Termini to Frascati.

① ★★ Frascati. The biggest but not the prettiest of the Castelli, Frascati is lively and has tons of restaurants and hole-in-the-wall *osterie* where townies (mostly old men) gather on rickety benches to sip the local *mescita* (rough-and-ready white wine, poured straight from great big wooden casks). Just below the town, adjacent to the train station, are the gardens and main house of the 17th-century **Villa Aldobrandini** (☎ 06-9420331), whose imposing, broken-pediment facade can be seen all the way from Rome's Janiculum Hill (p 59, bullet ⑪) on a clear day. The main building and gardens were designed by Giacomo della Porta and Carlo Maderno.

② ★★ Grottaferrata. Henry James wrote that this town "has nothing to charm the fond gazer but its situation"—high on a hill, with dramatic views over the Appian Way and Rome—"and its old fortified abbey," the wonderful 11th-century **Abbazia di San Nilo** (☎ 06-9459309), an example of medieval architecture rare for the Roman region.

③ ★★ Castelgandolfo. Overlooking volcanic Lake Albano, clean and elegant Castelgandolfo has been the popes' summer retreat since the 1500s—the 17th-century palace here is technically part of the Vatican. The town piazza has a fountain by Bernini, who also designed the Church of San Tommaso di Villanova, with its acrobatic stuccoes by Antonio Raggi.

④ ★★ Nemi. Set on the lip of an ancient volcanic crater, Nemi is by

A statue at the Villa Aldobrandini in Frascati.

far the most picturesque of the Castelli, and famous for its strawberries. Gorgeous Lake Nemi—formed by the water that collects in the crater—was called "Diana's Mirror" by the ancients because the surrounding woods seemed to suit the goddess of the hunt.

⑤ ★ Genzano. On the other side of the lake from Nemi, Genzano is at its best the week after Corpus Christi, when the streets are covered with flower petals for the *Infiorata* festival.

The town of **Ariccia** ⑥ is famous for *porchetta* (pork roast with garlic and rosemary). Stop for lunch at the wonderfully simple **Fraschetta dar Burino** (Via dell'Uccelliera 46-50; ☎ 333-1828584), where you can get a tasting menu of the local specialties, including wine, for 12€. *$$*.

Beaches & Etruscan Sites
Near Rome

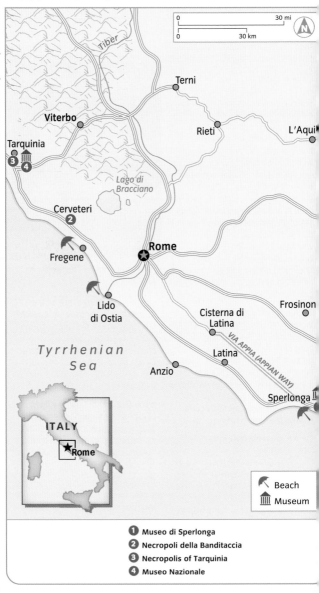

ITALY
★ Rome

Tyrrhenian Sea

Tiber

Terni

Viterbo

Rieti

L'Aqui

Tarquinia
3 4

Lago di Bracciano

Cerveteri
2

Fregene

Rome ★

Lido di Ostia

Cisterna di Latina

Frosinon

VIA APPIA (APPIAN WAY)

Latina

Anzio

Sperlonga

0 — 30 mi
0 — 30 km

🏖 Beach
🏛 Museum

1 Museo di Sperlonga
2 Necropoli della Banditaccia
3 Necropolis of Tarquinia
4 Museo Nazionale

The Roman *litorale* (seacoast) has never won any Mediterranean beauty contests, but there are several convenient and pleasant places to escape when summer in the city gets to be too much. When you tire of beachcombing, head north along the coast-hugging Via Aurelia to the ancient sites of Cerveteri and Tarquinia. Here you'll find fascinating physical evidence of the Etruscans, the sophisticated culture that ruled Italy before the Romans. Much of the jewelry and other finds from these cavernous painted tombs can be seen at Rome's Villa Giulia museum (p 30, bullet ②).

★ **Fregene.** The preferred seaside destination for upper-middle-class Romans, Fregene lies right below the path of jets on the final approach to Fiumicino airport. The topography isn't particularly gorgeous, but the see-and-be-seen crowd of super-bronzed bathers makes for quite a spectacle on its own. Go to beach-front **Il Mastino** (Via Silvi Marina 18; ☎ 06-434568) for an unforgettable lunch of spaghetti with clams. *COTRAL bus from Lepanto Metro station, about 1 hr.*

★★ **Sperlonga.** Well worth the trek from Rome, charming Sperlonga has two main beach areas. The crescent-shaped bay south of the point is the more picturesque, with wide swathes of sand. On the headlands above, Sperlonga town looks like a Greek village, with white-washed walls, narrow alleys, and spectacular vistas over the water. At the southern end of the bay is **Museo di Sperlonga** (☎ 0771-548028), with its marble sculptures of Polyphemus; and the attached, 2nd-century **Villa di Tiberio,** with its whimsical sea-grotto dining room. *Train to Fondi (D or R train toward Napoli), then bus to Sperlonga, about 1½ hr.*

★★ **Cerveteri.** Called Kysry by the Etruscans and Caere by the Romans, this town near the seacoast was one of Italy's great Etruscan cities and may date back as far as the 9th century B.C. It is home

The lovely beach at Sperlonga.

to the immensely atmospheric **Necropoli della Banditaccia,** whose labyrinth-like paths between thick trees and huge *tumulus* tombs feel like something out of an *Indiana Jones* adventure sequence. The typically Italian lax site supervision means you can clamber all over everything, which is great fun. ⏱ *1 hr. Via della Necropoli.* ☎ *06-9940001. 6€. Tues–Sun 8:30am–sunset. COTRAL bus from Cornelia Metro station to Cerveteri, about 1 hr.*

Ostia. Even if you have only half a day to spare, you can still make it to Ostia, Rome's closest seashore. The water here is far from sparkling, but it's lively, with plenty of beach clubs (and dark sand that Romans say accelerates tanning). At the ★★ *spiaggia libera,* or "free beach,"

A Day at the Beach

The beaches here, like in so many of the country's best places, are bustling with a deeply rooted social culture. **Beach clubs** *(stabilimenti)*—pleasant, and nearly identical—consume much of the coast near Rome, and typically charge between 10€ to 15€ for access to their shores; the daily fee includes a **lounge bed** *(lettino)* and **shade umbrella** *(ombrellone),* and use of changing rooms and shower facilities. Regardless of shape or age, about half of Italian women go topless at the beach, and half of the men wear Speedos. As for the water, while it's not exactly crystalline near Rome, it's plenty clean for swimming—and no matter where you go, you'll find take-out huts serving delicious cold-mozzarella-and-tomato sandwiches or plates of steaming pasta with fresh Mediterranean seafood.

bus no. 7 from Cristoforo Colombo train station takes you to rugged dunes and wider stretches of sand, which make for a much more attractive setting, but there are few facilities. *Train from Porta San Paolo (Piramide Metro station) to Ostia Centro, Stella Polare, or Cristoforo Colombo, about 35 min.*

★★ Tarquinia. The **necropolis** of Tarquinia may not be as lush or ancient-feeling as the one at Cerveteri, but the tombs here have vivid, beautifully preserved wall paintings. In the town, the **Museo Nazionale** (located in the noble Palazzo Vitelleschi) houses prized terra-cotta winged horses from the 4th century B.C., among the greatest Etruscan masterpieces ever found, as well as exhibits and sarcophagi excavated from the necropolis. Tarquinia itself is a very pretty medieval town, with several good restaurants. ⏲ *2½ hr. (necropolis and museum).* ☎ *0766-856036. 6.50€ for both sites. Necropolis Tues–Sun 8:30am–1 hr. before sunset; museum 8:30am–7:30pm. COTRAL bus from Cornelia Metro station to Civitavecchia, then change buses to Tarquinia, about 2 hr.* ●

Inside the Necropoli at Cerveteri.

The
Savvy Traveler

Before You Go

Government Tourist Offices

In the U.S.: 630 Fifth Ave., Ste. 1565, New York, NY 10111 (☎ 212/245-4822); 500 N. Michigan Ave., Ste. 2240, Chicago, IL 60611 (☎ 312/644-0996); and 12400 Wilshire Blvd., Ste. 550, Los Angeles, CA 90025 (☎ 310/820-1898). **In Canada:** 175 Bloor St. E., South Tower, Ste. 907, Toronto, ONT, M4W 3R8 (☎ 020/7408-1254). **In the U.K. & Ireland:** 1 Princes St., London, W1B 2AY (☎ 020/7408-1254; www.italiantouristboard.co.uk). **In Australia:** Level 4, 46 Market St., Sydney, NSW 2000 (☎ 02/9262-1666).

The Best Times to Go

April to June and late September to October are the best months to travel in Italy. Starting in mid-June, the summer rush really picks up, and from July to mid-September the country teems with visitors. August is the worst month for touring: It can get uncomfortably hot, muggy, and crowded, and the entire country goes on vacation at least from August 15 to the end of the month (many Italians take off the entire month). Many hotels, restaurants, and shops are closed (except at the spas, beaches, and islands, which are where 70% of the Italians head). From late October to Easter, most attractions go on shorter winter hours or are closed for renovation. Many hotels and restaurants take a month or two off between November and February, spa and beach destinations become padlocked ghost towns, and it can get much colder than you'd expect (it might even snow).

Previous page: Riding through the streets of Rome.

Festivals & Special Events

SPRING. The 42km (26 miles) of the **Maratona di Roma** are run the 3rd Sunday in March. During the **Settimana dei Beni Culturali** 1 week in April (www.beniculturali.it), admission is free to many museums and monuments. In late March and early April, azaleas cover the Spanish Steps in the **Mostra delle Azalee. Settimana Santa (Holy Week)** and **Pasqua (Easter)** in March or April are the biggest Catholic holidays of the year, with the pope partaking in dramatic ceremonies daily. Every April 21, Rome celebrates its birthday **(Natale di Roma)** with fireworks over the Campidoglio. Workers' unions organize a huge free rock concert at San Giovanni on **Primo Maggio** (May 1). The **Italian Open** brings the VIPs of the world tennis circuit to the Foro Italico (the Forum) for 10 days in May. Firemen pour buckets of rose petals over the heads of the congregation at the Pantheon on **Pentecost.**

SUMMER. **Estate Romana** (June–Aug) brings concerts to the sites of ruins, and open-air cinemas to piazzas. The miraculous snowfall of August 5, A.D. 352, is reenacted every year in Santa Maria Maggiore with a flurry of white flower petals during the **Festa della Madonna della Neve.** Get out of town, or wish you had, on **Ferragosto** (beginning Aug 15)—a 2-week holiday when *everyone* in Rome takes a vacation.

FALL. The pope says Mass at the Verano Cemetery on **Ognissanti (All Saints' Day),** November 1. For the **Giornata dei Defunti (Day of the Dead)** on November 2, Romans visit the graves of family members.

ROME'S AVERAGE DAILY TEMPERATURE & MONTHLY RAINFALL

	JAN	FEB	MAR	APR	MAY	JUNE
Temp. (°F)	49	52	57	62	72	82
Temp. (°C)	9	11	14	17	22	28
Rainfall (in.)	2.3	1.5	2.9	3.0	2.8	2.9

	JULY	AUG	SEPT	OCT	NOV	DEC
Temp. (°F)	87	86	73	65	56	47
Temp. (°C)	31	30	23	20	13	8
Rainfall (in.)	1.5	1.9	2.8	2.6	3.0	2.1

WINTER. To celebrate the **Immacolata Concezione** (Dec 8), firemen shimmy up a column in Piazza di Spagna to place a wreath on the arm of the Virgin Mary. Nativity scenes *(presepi)* spring up all over town in the weeks leading to **Natale (Christmas).** Italians ring in **Capodanno (New Year's)** by partying in the streets, setting off fireworks, and casting unwanted furniture out windows. On January 5, a witch called **La Befana** "lands" at Piazza Navona, signifying the arrival of **Epiphany** (Jan 6) and the end of the holiday season.

Weather

Rome's generally mild climate means that you can enjoy visiting the city year-round, and can eat dinner outside April through October. Summer (especially late July and Aug) can be hot and humid, making for less-than-ideal touring weather. May and October are generally the best months for sightseeing, with sunny days, temperatures between 60° and 80°F (15°–26°C), and beautiful light. March is often rainy, and November brings the first bite of autumn. January and February are the coldest months, though winter temperatures rarely drop below 40°F (4°C).

Useful Websites

- **www.adr.com**: Information about Rome's airports.

- **www.romaturismo.com**: The official site of the Rome tourist board, with tons of info on monuments, museums, and cultural events, downloadable brochures, and a searchable database for accommodations.

- **www.museidiroma.com**: Information about Rome's museums (not exhaustive, and in Italian only).

- **www.trenitalia.com**: Schedules, fares, and online booking for the national train system.

- **www.vatican.va**: The Vatican's excellent official site; see also the comprehensive site for the Vatican Museums at http://mv.vatican.va.

- **www.wantedinrome.com**: Rome's main expatriate publication has a good online classified section; otherwise, content is mediocre.

- **www.weather.com**: Up-to-the-minute worldwide weather reports.

Cellphones

World phones are the only U.S. phones that can be used in Italy. Italy (like most other countries) is on the GSM (Global System for Mobiles) wireless network. GSM phones function with a removable plastic SIM card, encoded with your phone number and account information.

In Italy, you can buy an inexpensive phone and SIM card for about 100€ and buy prepaid minutes in increments of 5€ to 20€.

You can also rent one in the U.S. before leaving home from **InTouch USA** (☎ 800/872-7626; www.intouchglobal.com), **RoadPost** (☎ 888/290-1606 or 905/272-5665; www.roadpost.com), or **Cellhire** (www.cellhire.com, www.cellhire.co.uk, www.cellhire.com.au).

U.K. mobiles all work in Italy; call your service provider before departing your home country to ensure that the international call bar has been switched off and to check call charges, which can be extremely high. Also remember that you are charged for calls you *receive* on a U.K. mobile used abroad.

Car Rentals

All roads might lead to Rome, but you don't want to drive once you get here. Because the reception desks of most Roman hotels have at least one English-speaking person, call ahead to ask about the best route into Rome from your starting point. You're usually allowed to park in front of the hotel long enough to

unload your luggage. You'll want to get rid of your rental car as soon as possible or park it in a garage.

You can opt to use the rental car to explore the countryside around Rome or to drive to another city. You'll save the most money if you reserve a car before leaving your home country. Over the past several years, I've found AutoEuropa (**www.sbc.it**) to have the best online rental deals in Italy. If you want to book a car in Rome, all the agencies have desks inside Termini station and Fiumicino airport as well as city center locations in the vicinity of Via Veneto and Villa Borghese. **AutoEuropa** is at Via Calabria 11 (☎ 06-42019014), **Hertz** is on Viale del Muro Torto, in the underground parking lot of the Villa Borghese (☎ 06-3216831); and **Avis** is at Via Sardegna 38a (☎ 06-42824728). **Maggiore,** another Italian company, has an office at Via Po 8a (☎ 06-8548698).

From the U.K., I recommend **www.holidayautos.co.uk**. All prepaid vouchers include insurance—which can be astronomical in Italy. Book online with them for the minimum guaranteed £10 discount.

Getting **There**

By Plane

Chances are you'll arrive at Rome's **Leonardo da Vinci International Airport** (☎ 06-65951 or 06-65953640), popularly known as Fiumicino, 30km (19 miles) from the city center. (If you're flying by charter, you might land at Ciampino Airport, discussed below.)

After you leave Passport Control, you'll see two **information desks** (one for Rome, one for Italy; ☎ 06-65954471). At the Rome desk, you can pick up a general map and

pamphlets Monday through Saturday from 8:15am to 7pm. The staff can help you find a hotel room if you haven't reserved ahead. A **cambio** (money exchange) operates daily from 7:30am to 11pm, offering surprisingly good rates.

There's a **train station** in the airport. To get into the city, follow the signs marked TRENI for the 30-minute express train to Rome's main station, **Stazione Termini** (arriving on Track 22). The shuttle runs from 6:37am to 11:37pm for 11€

one-way. On the way, you'll pass a yellow machine dispensing tickets (cash or credit), or you can buy them from the news agent (cash only) near the tracks. When you arrive at Termini, get out of the train quickly and grab a baggage cart. (It's a long schlep from the track to the exit or to the other train connections, and baggage carts can be scarce.) Do watch out for pickpockets at Termini—they love to prey on fresh and disoriented new arrivals.

A **taxi** from Fiumicino airport to the city costs 40€ (the new fixed rate introduced in 2007) for the 30-minute to 1-hour trip, depending on traffic. The expense might be worth it if you have a lot of luggage or don't want to bother taking a train. There are always plenty of metered, white, official Comune di Roma cabs outside the terminal. Note that the flat rate of 40€ is applicable from the airport to central Rome and vice versa, but only if your central Rome location is inside the Aurelian Walls (most hotels are). Otherwise, standard metered rates apply, which can be 10€ higher.

If you arrive on a charter or low-cost flight at **Ciampino Airport** (☎ **06-794941**), you can take the **Terravision** coach (☎ **06-79341722;** 8€) to Termini. Alternatively, the **Sit Bus Shuttle** (☎ **06-5916826**) between Ciampino to Termini runs every 30 to 60 minutes and costs 6€. A **taxi** from this airport to Rome costs 30€, a flat rate that applies as long as you're going to a destination within the old Aurelian Walls. Otherwise, you'll pay the metered fare.

By Car
From the north, the main access route is **Autostrada del Sole (A1),** which cuts through Milan and Florence; or you can take the coastal route, **SSI Aurelia,** from Genoa. If you're driving north from Naples, you take the southern lap of **Autostrada del Sole (A2).** All the autostradas join with the **Grande Raccordo Anulare,** a ring road encircling Rome and channeling traffic into the congested city. Long before you reach this road, you should study a map carefully to see what part of Rome you plan to enter, and mark your route accordingly. Route markings along the ring road tend to be confusing. **Important:** Return your rental car immediately, or at least get yourself to a hotel, park your car, and leave it there until you leave Rome. Don't even try to drive in Rome—the traffic is just too nightmarish.

By Train, Bus, or Metro
Trains and buses (including trains from the airport) arrive in the center of old Rome at **Stazione Termini,** Piazza dei Cinquecento (☎ **892021**); this is the train, bus, and Metro transportation hub for all of Rome and is surrounded by many hotels (especially cheaper ones).

If you're taking the **Metropolitana,** follow the illuminated red-and-white M signs. To catch a **bus,** go straight through the station's outer hall to the sprawling bus lot of Piazza dei Cinquecento. You'll find **taxis** there as well. Note that taxis now charge a 2€ supplement for any fares originating at Termini. This is official city policy, though not well-marked, so don't feel that you're getting ripped off.

The station is filled with services. At a branch of the Banca San Paolo IMI (at Tracks 1 and 24), you can exchange money. **Informazioni Ferroviarie** (in the outer hall) dispenses information on rail travel to other parts of Italy. There's also a **tourist information booth** here, along with baggage services, newsstands, and snack bars.

Getting **Around**

By Car
Don't drive in the center of Rome. Period.

By Taxi
Licensed taxis are white or, less commonly, yellow. Be sure your cab has the red SPQR insignia on the driver's door. Cabs can be difficult to hail on the street, particularly during the day. Always insist on the metered fare, never an arranged price. The meter starts at 2.33€ from 7am to 10pm Monday to Saturday, and at 4.91€ from 10pm to 7am every day. On Sunday and holidays from 7am to 10pm, the meter starts at 3.36€. As a guideline, a daytime fare between Termini and the Vatican (one of the longer distances in the city center) should be15€ to 20€, depending of traffic. Add the tip by rounding up to the next whole euro—if the fare is 7.40€, leave the driver 8€.

By Metro
The **Metropolitana,** or **Metro,** for short, is the fastest means of transportation, operating daily from 5:30am to 11:30pm. A big red M indicates the entrance.

Tickets are 1€ and are available from *tabacchi* (tobacco shops, most of which display a sign with a white T on a brown background), many newsstands, and vending machines at all stations. Some stations have managers, but they won't make change. Booklets of tickets are available at *tabacchi* and in some terminals. You can also buy **passes** for 1 to 7 days (see "By Bus & Tram," below).

Building an underground transportation system for Rome hasn't been easy because every time workers start digging, they discover an old temple or other archaeological treasure, and heavy earth-moving has to cease for a while.

By Bus & Tram
Roman buses and trams are operated by an organization known as **ATAC** (Azienda Tramvie e Autobus del Comune di Roma), Via Volturno 65 (☎ **800-431784** for information).

For 1€ you can ride to most parts of Rome, although it can be slow going in all that traffic, and the buses are often very crowded. Your ticket is valid for 75 minutes, and you can get on many buses and trams (as well as the Metro) during that time by using the same ticket. Ask your hotel where to buy bus tickets, or buy them in *tabacchi* or at bus terminals. You must have your ticket before boarding because there are no ticket-issuing machines on the vehicles.

At Stazione Termini, you can buy a **1-day ticket** *(biglietto giornaliero),* which costs 4€, or a **weekly ticket** *(biglietto settimanale "carta"),* which costs 16€. These passes allow you to ride the ATAC network without buying individual tickets. A **tourist pass** costs 11€ and is valid for 3 days. The tourist pass, the 1-day ticket, and the weekly tickets are valid on buses, trams, and the Metro—but never ride the trains when the Romans are going to or from work, or you'll be smashed flatter than fettuccine. On the first bus you board, you place your ticket in a small machine, which prints the day and hour you boarded, and then you withdraw it.

Buses and trams stop at areas marked FERMATA. At most of these, a yellow sign displays the numbers of the buses that stop there and lists all the stops along each bus's route in order, so you can easily search out your destination. In general, they're in service daily from 6am to midnight. After that and until dawn, you can ride on special night buses (they have an N in front of their bus number), which run only on main routes, and only once an hour. It's best to take a taxi in the wee hours—if you can find one.

At the **bus information booth** at Piazza dei Cinquecento, in front of the Stazione Termini, you can purchase a directory complete with maps summarizing the bus routes.

Although routes change often, a few reliable ones have remained valid for years, such as **no. 75** from Stazione Termini to the Colosseum, **H** from Stazione Termini to Trastevere, and **no. 40** from Stazione Termini to the Vatican. But if you're

going somewhere and are dependent on the bus, be sure to carefully check where the bus stop is and exactly which bus goes there on what day. Your hotel staff should also be able to give you the lowdown on buses in your particular neighborhood.

On Foot

Seeing the city on foot (and getting a little lost while you're at it) is the best way to get oriented. Many main sights are very close together, and the *centro* is mostly flat (the seven hills are elsewhere). A walk from the Pantheon to the Spanish Steps, for instance, takes only 10 to 15 minutes and is packed with things to see.

Fast **Facts**

APARTMENT RENTALS   For short-term vacation rentals in Rome—a fantastic and money-saving way to experience the city—check out **Roman Reference** (www.romanreference.com), **Rental in Rome** (www.rentalinrome. com), or **Rome-Accom** (www.rome-accom.com). For longer stays, see the classifieds in the English-language magazine **Wanted in Rome** at its website (www.wanted inrome.com/clas) or at newsstands. The most comprehensive (and overwhelming) classified newspaper for long-term room or apartment rentals is the Italian-only **Porta Portese,** at its website (www.porta portese.it) or at newsstands.

ATMS/CASHPOINTS   The easiest way to get euros is at an ATM (or cashpoint), using your bank or credit card. Keep in mind that credit card companies charge interest from the day of your withdrawal, even if you

pay your monthly bill on time. There are **ATMs (bancomat)** all over central Rome; you'll be charged at least a 3€ fee (in addition to whatever your home bank charges for international withdrawals). Cash tends to run out by Saturday night and isn't replenished until Monday afternoon, so think ahead. Also, find out your daily limit before you leave home.

BABYSITTING   Most mid- to upper-range hotels can arrange babysitting services; otherwise, call the American Women's Association (☎ 06-4825268) for a list of reliable sitters. The Angels agency (☎ 06-6782877), run by Brit Rebecca Harden, arranges English-speaking nannies for wealthy Italian families and can help you, too.

BANKING HOURS   Teller windows are open Monday to Friday from 8:45am to 1:30pm and from 2:45 to 4pm. Queues can be painfully slow.

B&BS The **Bed & Breakfast Italia** agency, Corso Vittorio Emanuele 284 (☎ **06-6878618;** www.bbitalia. it), has a dizzying array of accommodations, ranging from private apartments in historic *palazzi* to more spartan sleeps with shared bathrooms. Rates range from 25€ to 80€ per person per night. **My Home Your Home,** Lungotevere dei Mellini 35 (☎ **06-97613280;** www.myhomeyourhome.it), has fewer but more luxurious listings. Rates are 100€ to 200€ per person per night.

BIKE RENTALS Rome's busy, Vespa-infested streets are not especially bicycle-friendly, but the parks make for good riding, and Sundays are largely traffic-free and pleasant city-wide. Just outside the entrance to the Spagna Metro station, **Spagna Rent,** Vicolo del Bottino (☎ **339-4277773**), rents bikes by the hour or the day, convenient for riding in the Villa Borghese nearby. **Tranchina,** Via Cavour 80 (☎ **06-4815669;** www.scooterhire.it), between Termini and the Colosseum, rents bikes as well as mopeds.

BUSINESS & SHOP HOURS Most Roman shops open at 10am and close at 7pm from Monday to Saturday, closing for 1 or 2 hours at lunch. Designer boutiques, chain stores, and shops in heavily touristed areas do not close for lunch and are open Sunday. Smaller shops are often closed Monday morning and Saturday afternoon. Most restaurants are closed for *riposo* (rest) 1 day per week, usually Sunday or Monday.

CLIMATE See "Weather," p 161.

CONCERTS See "Tickets," below.

CONSULATES & EMBASSIES **United States Consulate and Embassy,** Via Veneto 119 (☎ 06-46741; www. usembassy.it). **Canadian Consulate,** Via Zara 30 (☎ 06/445-981; www. canada.it). **British Embassy,** Via XX Settembre 80 (☎ 06-42200001;

www.britain.it). **Australian Embassy,** Via Antonio Bosio 5 (☎ 06-852721; www.italy.embassy.gov.au).

CREDIT CARDS Credit cards are a safe way to carry money. They also provide a convenient record of all your expenses, and they generally offer good exchange rates. You can also withdraw cash advances from your credit cards at banks or ATMs (Cashpoints), provided you know your PIN. If you've forgotten yours, or didn't even know you had one, call the number on the back of your credit card and ask the bank to send it to you. It usually takes 5 to 7 business days, though some banks will provide the number over the phone if you tell them your mother's maiden name or some other personal information. Keep in mind that when you use your credit card abroad, most banks assess a 2% fee above the 1% fee charged by Visa, MasterCard, or American Express for currency conversion on credit charges. But credit cards still may be the smart way to go when you factor in things like exorbitant ATM fees and higher traveler's check exchange rates (as well as service fees).

CUSTOMS Customs *(dogana)* at Italian airports tends to be lax; unless you're carrying a great deal of luggage or look suspicious, no one will bother to inspect you as you clear the arrivals area. By law, anyone arriving from outside the E.U. is allowed to bring up to 200 cigarettes, two bottles of wine, and one bottle of liquor into Italy, duty-free. There are no limits for anyone, foreign nationals included, arriving from another E.U. country. File through the "Blue Exit" lane at Customs.

DENTISTS See "Emergencies," below.

DINING Breakfast in Rome traditionally consists of a cappuccino and pastry at the local bar, not a full, sit-down meal, though most hotels offer some kind of continental breakfast. Cafes and snack bars are typically open 6:30am to 8pm, later in tourist areas; many are closed on Sunday. Restaurants are open for lunch 12:30 to 3pm, and for dinner 7:30 to 11:30pm (the last seating is usually at 10:30pm). Attire has gotten more casual at Roman restaurants in recent years. Jeans are acceptable almost everywhere—but shorts are frowned upon, except in really touristy areas.

Most informal Roman restaurants will accept reservations, but they're often not necessary, particularly if you arrive around 8pm (arrive earlier and you'll be dining alone). More formal restaurants do require reservations. You should contact your concierge at the time that you book a room, and ask him to book a table (you can tip him on arrival). Children are generally welcome everywhere.

DOCTORS See "Emergencies," below.

ELECTRICITY Like most of continental Europe, Italy uses the 220-volt system (two round prongs). American (110-volt) electronics with dual voltage (laptops and shavers) can be used with a simple adapter. Other appliances like hair dryers require a clunky voltage converter; using such appliances with simple adapters (not converters) will most likely fry the appliance and blow fuses. U.K. 240-volt appliances need a continental adaptor, widely available at home but impossible to find in Italy.

EMBASSIES See "Consulates & Embassies," above.

EMERGENCIES Italy has several emergency phone numbers: The *Polizia* are at ☎ 112; the *carabinieri* (they speak more English than the regular police), ☎ 113. Call ☎ 115 for the **fire department.** For an **ambulance,** call ☎ 118. Emergency care in Roman hospitals is efficient—and free for all foreign citizens. U.K. nationals should ensure they have a completed and validated E111 form to receive full health benefits in Italy. Visitors will need the European Health Insurance Card to receive free treatment. For advice, ask at your local post office or see www.dh.gov.uk/travellers. Should you find yourself in need of medical attention, ask to go to the nearest *pronto soccorso* (emergency room). Hospitals abound in Rome, though **Ospedale Fatebenefratelli** on Tiber Island, Piazza Fatebenefratelli 2 (☎ 06-68371), is one of the best. For dental emergencies, head for **Ospedale Dentistico George Eastman,** in the Policlinico medical complex at Viale Regina Elena 287B (☎ 06-844831). **Ospedale Bambino Gesù,** Piazza Sant'Onofrio 4 (☎ 06-68591), on the Gianicolo, is central Italy's premier pediatric hospital.

EVENT LISTINGS The weekly *Roma C'e* (1.20€ at newsstands) has the most thorough listings for concerts, theater, dance, opera, movies, guided tours, and other happenings. There's a small English section in back. The "Roma" sections of the daily newspapers *Corriere della Sera, La Repubblica,* and *Il Messaggero* list major events.

FAMILY TRAVEL Italian hotels and restaurants are generally very accommodating to children. Rome's many city parks (p 92) offer respite from the stress of sightseeing in a chaotic urban environment. See also "Babysitting," above.

GAY & LESBIAN TRAVELERS **Circolo Mario Mieli di Cultura Omosessuale** (☎ 06-5413985; www.mariomieli.org) is the best gay and lesbian resource in Rome. **Arcigay** (☎ 06-8555522; www.arcigay.it) and **ArciLesbica** (☎ 06-4180369) offer political and recreational forums and phone help lines.

HEALTH CLUBS Day memberships are offered at the **Roman Sports Center,** at the Villa Borghese underground parking structure (☎ 06-3201667); and at **Fitness First,** at Termini station/Via Giolitti 44 (☎ 06-47826300). Single yoga and Pilates classes are offered at **Moves,** Via dei Coronari 46 (☎ 06-6864989), near Piazza Navona.

HOLIDAYS Celebrated in Rome are New Year's Day (Jan 1); Epiphany (Jan 6); Easter and Easter Monday (Mar or Apr); Liberation Day (Apr 25); Labor Day (May 1); St. Peter's Day (June 29, Rome only); Ferragosto (Aug 15); All Saints' Day (Nov 1); Immaculate Conception (Dec 8); Christmas (Dec 25); and St. Stephen's Day (Dec 26). Shops and most restaurants are closed, and it can be very difficult to find accommodations in Rome over these holiday weekends.

INSURANCE Check your existing insurance policies and credit card coverage before buying travel insurance. You may already be covered for lost luggage, cancelled tickets, or medical expenses. If you aren't covered, expect to pay between 5% and 8% of your trip's cost for insurance. For trip-cancellation and lost-luggage insurance, try **Travel Guard International** (☎ 800/826-4919; www.travelguard.com) or **Travel Insured International** (☎ 800/243-3174; www.travel insured.com). North Americans interested in getting medical insurance, including emergency evacuation coverage, can contact **Travel Assistance International** (☎ 800/821-2828; www.travelassistance. com). **For U.K. citizens,** insurance is always advisable, even if you have form E111 (see "Emergencies," above). Travelers, or families who make more than one trip abroad per year, may find an annual travel insurance policy works out to be cheaper. Check www.moneysuper market.com, which compares prices across a wide range of providers for single- and multi-trip policies.

INTERNET Most Roman hotels have Internet access—dial-up or broadband connections in guest rooms, a hotel-wide wireless network, or an Internet terminal in the lobby. Otherwise, most areas have a small Internet/phone center where you can pay about 4€ an hour to log on. For those with laptops, there are a few "hotspots" (wireless networks)—many parts of the Villa Borghese have free Wi-Fi (though you have to have a valid local mobile number to register); the Internet cafe/tearoom **Gran Caffè La Caffettiera,** Piazza di Pietra 65 (☎ 06/679-8147), near the Pantheon, has great atmosphere.

LIMOS Try **Bob's Limousines & Tours** (☎ 06-5211192; www.rome limousines.com); or try **RomaLimo** (☎ 06-5414663; www.romalimo. com).

LOST PROPERTY Always file a police report if you wish to submit an insurance claim. Items left on buses and Metros, or at other city-run agencies, may turn up at the **Oggetti Smarriti (Lost Objects)** office in Trastevere at Via Bettoni 1 (☎ 06-5816040). For property left on trains, try the Oggetti Smarriti desk at Termini station (near platform 24).

MAIL & POSTAGE STAMPS Stamps *(francobolli)* for the *Poste Italiane* can be purchased at post offices or at most tobacco shops *(tabacchi)* and hotel reception desks. Though the national mail has made vast improvements in recent years, many still swear by the Vatican mail. The *Poste Vaticane* has offices and mail drops only in Vatican City; postage costs the same as the Italian mail postage.

MONEY Italy's currency is the euro (at press time, equal to $1.55/£.79).

The best way to get cash in Rome is at ATMs or Cashpoints (above). While credit cards are accepted at almost all shops, restaurants, and hotels, always have some cash on hand for incidentals and sightseeing admissions. For the most up-to-date currency conversion information, go to www.xe.com.

OPTICIANS   Eyeglasses can be repaired and contact lenses can be purchased (no written prescription required) at any *ottica* (optician's), also the only place to buy contact lens solution.

PARKING   You don't want to drive a car once you're in Rome. Finding street parking is a nightmare in the city center, and parking laws are beyond confusing. Either turn in your rental car once you arrive or, if you plan to take a number of day trips while you're there, consider parking at the **ParkSi** underground lot at Villa Borghese, Via del Galoppatoio 33 (☎ 06-3225934).

PASSES   Rome does not have a fully comprehensive sightseeing pass, but the new **RomaPass** (www.roma pass.it; 20€ for 3 days) gets you free admission for two sites (most museums and monuments are covered), plus discounts on subsequent admissions as well as free city public transportation. For 5€ more, the **Roma&Più pass** includes free travel on regional buses and trains and discounts on regional attractions (good if you're planning on day trips) but does *not* cover the airport buses and trains. For Rome's major archaeological sites, one 11€ ticket gets you into the Colosseum, the Roman Forum (which was free until 2008), and the Palatine, but it must be used within 48 hours. The archaeological superintendency also offers a 7-day **Roma Archeologia pass** (20€) that includes admission to the Colosseum, Roman Forum, Palatine, Baths of Caracalla,

all three locations of the Museo Nazionale Romano, and Crypta Balbi, as well as Villa dei Quintili and the Tomb of Cecilia Metella on the Appian Way. The pass can be purchased at any of the above sites; it pays off if you visit three or more sites. The 6€ **Appia Antica card** is good for 7 days and includes the Baths of Caracalla, the Tomb of Cecilia Metella, and the Villa of the Quintili (though not any of the catacombs, which are under the Church's jurisdiction).

PASSPORTS   Always keep a photocopy of your passport with you when you're traveling. If your passport is lost or stolen, having a copy significantly facilitates the reissuing process at your consulate. While in Rome, keep your passport and other valuables in your room's safe or in the hotel safe *(cassaforte)*. See "Consulates & Embassies," above, for more information.

PHARMACIES   *Farmacie* are recognizable by their neon green or red cross signs. They are the only places to buy over-the-counter medications like ibuprofen or cough syrup. Most pharmacies can fill prescriptions from home (some will even do so without a written prescription). A few pharmacies, like those at Piazza Cinquecento 49–53 and at Via Nazionale 228, are open late. Pharmacy hours are confusing, but all pharmacies, when closed, have signs in their windows indicating the addresses of open pharmacies in the area.

SAFETY   Violent crime is virtually nonexistent, but petty theft and scams can be a problem. Pickpockets, some of them Gypsies, expertly work the tourist areas, crowded buses, and Termini station. Men should not carry wallets in back pockets, and women should carry handbags close to their bodies, securely fastened. Petty thieves do not prey on locals, so attitude and awareness will keep you from being targeted. Gypsies normally travel in groups of two or three, with babies slung across their chests. Other pickpockets dress like typical businesspeople and can be harder to spot. Always be suspicious of any individual who goes out of his or her way to "befriend" you in a densely touristed area. In general, Rome is quite safe—walking alone at night is usually fine anywhere in the *centro storico*. For more information, consult the U.S. State Department's website at www.travel.state.gov; in the U.K., consult the Foreign Office's website, www.fco.gov.uk; and in Australia, consult the government travel advisory service at www. smartraveller.gov.au.

SCOOTER RENTALS   The best way to "do as the Romans do" is to rent a scooter. Just show respect for pedestrians and other drivers in the chaotic city traffic, and go slowly until you get the hang of it. You'll find agencies in all the tourist areas (or ask at your hotel)—expect to pay between 40€ and 50€ per day for a scooter. An agency I like is **RomaRent,** Vicolo dei Bovari 7A (☎ 06-6896555; www.romarent.net).

SENIOR TRAVELERS   Non-E.U. seniors are entitled to precious few discounts while in Rome, although AARP (☎ 800/424-3410) members can save on airfare and car rentals arranged prior to departure. **Elderhostel** (☎ 877/426-8056) organizes well-priced "study trips" to many world destinations from the U.S., including Italy; the courses are geared toward active seniors, and accommodations may be spartan.

SMOKING   On January 10, 2005, a revolutionary nationwide smoking ban went into effect in bars and restaurants. Amazingly enough, the legislation stuck, and no one smokes inside anymore. You can still puff away at sidewalk tables.

SPECTATOR SPORTS   One of the best experiences you can have in modern Rome is going to a **Roma** or **Lazio** football (soccer) game at the Stadio Olimpico (p 132). Tickets go on sale 6 days before games and cost 20€ to 100€. The season runs from late August or early September to May or June.

TAXES   Non-E.U. visitors (with the exception of citizens from the U.K. and Ireland) who spend 155€ or more at stores with TAX-FREE stickers are entitled to a VAT refund (up to 13% of the total purchase amount). The cashier will fill out a form, which you must present at the Customs office at the **last European point** of departure (for example, the Amsterdam airport, if you're flying to the U.S. with a connection in Amsterdam). Cash refunds are given in euros, which must then be changed. Credit card refunds can take from 6 months to be processed.

TAXIS   It's usually (but not always) impossible to hail a taxi on the street. During busy hours, they're required by law to pick up fares only at taxi stands at the center of Rome, Piazza Venezia (east side), Piazza di Spagna (Spanish Steps), the Colosseum, Corso Rinascimento (Piazza Navona), Largo Argentina, the Pantheon, Piazza del Popolo, Piazza Risorgimento (near St. Peter's), and Piazza Belli (Trastevere). Taxis can also be requested by phone (☎ 06-3570, 06-88177, 06-6645, 06-4185, 06-4994)—the meter starts from the moment your cab is dispatched. Note that the taxi companies will ask you to call again later if they can't guarantee a cab within 13 minutes. Early morning taxis to the airport can also be reserved in advance, at no extra charge, and are generally reliable. Fares within the city typically range from 6€ to

20€. Fare to or from the airport costs 40€ (flat rate to and from Fiumicino) or 30€ (flat rate to and from Ciampino). **Note:** The fixed airport fares are only valid if your city destination or point of origin is inside the old Aurelian Walls (Mura Aureliane)—otherwise, the metered rate applies. If you're not sure, check with your driver.

TELEPHONES   Italy phased out its coin phones long ago. Phone booths *(la cabina)* take the *scheda telefonica* (plastic phone card) only, sold in denominations of 2.50€, 5€, and 7.75€ at *tabacchi*. Break off the perforated corner, and insert the card to get a dial tone. (Even if you have a prepaid long-distance calling card, you must insert a *scheda telefonica* to open the line.) Local calls (beginning with 06) usually cost 10¢ to 20¢; calls to Italian cell phones (beginning with 328, 338, 339, 340, 347, 348, and so forth) are wildly expensive—more than 1€ per minute.

TICKETS   For concert and theater tickets, visit the venue box office or the **Orbis** agency, Piazza Esquilino 37 (☎ 06-4827403). For soccer tickets, go to the Roma Store, Lazio Point (p 131), or a **Lottomatica** (located inside many, but not all, *tabacchi*). Your hotel concierge may be able to help you; ask when you book your room (and offer a tip).

TIPPING   Many Roman waiters have grown accustomed to receiving gratuities of 15% from tourists, but Italians don't tip nearly that much, and waiters don't depend on them to feed their families. In general, rounding up a lunch or dinner bill is sufficient. (If, say, the check is 33€, leave 35€.) Check to see if the *servizio* is included; if it is, no additional gratuity is necessary. At the coffee bar, always add a few coins when you place your order (10¢ is perfectly acceptable, but 20¢ will get you faster service).

In hotels, a service charge of 15% to 19% is already added to the bill, but it's customary to give a small gratuity (50¢/day) to the chambermaid. You should tip a porter a few euros for each bag carried to your room. A helpful concierge should also get a tip. Taxi drivers should be tipped about 10% of the fare, more if heavy baggage lifting is involved.

TOILETS   City-maintained public toilets are rare; those that do exist are often far from sanitary. Cafes, bars, and restaurants are required by law to let even non-customers use their restrooms, so don't be shy; just ask politely for the *bagno*.

TOURIST OFFICES   The state-operated tourist bureau, or **APT,** Via Parigi 5 (☎ 06-36004399; www. romaturismo.com), provides maps, pamphlets, and other info. Much more helpful and friendly is the private tourist agency **Enjoy Rome,** at Via Marghera 8A (☎ 06-4451843; www.enjoyrome.com), which also gives out free maps and a city guide and arranges tours.

TOURIST TRAPS   Avoid restaurants with menus in eight languages, and—sad to say—any restaurant on a major tourist square such as Piazza Navona. Other tourist traps are the so-called "architecture/history/Latin students" who offer free tours in popular monuments (see "Tours," below). See also "Safety," above.

TOURS   Rome has plenty of tour companies, but I recommend **Enjoy Rome,** Via Marghera 8A (☎ 06-4451843; www.enjoyrome.com), which offers a wide range of educational and entertaining group and private walking tours, bike tours, and bus tours. Guides are expats educated in art and history, or licensed Italian guides and archaeologists. For a more in-depth, academic experience, the specialized, small-group tours organized by **Context Rome** (☎ 888-467-1986 toll-free from the U.S., ☎ 06-4820911 in Italy, www.contextrome.com) are outstanding. **Note:** People offering "free tours" at places like the Forum and St. Peter's are often unqualified hacks.

TRAVELERS WITH DISABILITIES   Many *centro storico* hotels and some lesser sites remain inaccessible to wheelchairs; call to inquire. The **COIN** agency, Via Enrico Giglioli 54A (☎ 06-23267504; www.coinsociale.it/tourism), provides up-to-date information about wheelchair accessibility at hotels, restaurants, monuments, and museums.

VAT   See "Taxes," above.

A Brief History

6TH–5TH CENTURIES B.C. Following the expulsion of the seventh king of Rome, the Roman Republic begins. Roman law is codified in 450 B.C.

3RD CENTURY B.C. Rome defeats Carthage in the Punic Wars, opening the way for Mediterranean expansion.

2ND CENTURY B.C. Rome conquers Greece and adopts the Greek gods.

50S B.C. Caesar invades Britain and conquers Gaul (France).

44 B.C. Julius Caesar is assassinated on the Ides of March.

31 B.C. Octavian (Augustus) defeats Antony and Cleopatra at Actium, annexing Egypt.

A.D. 41 Caligula is assassinated; Claudius is emperor until he is poisoned in A.D. 54.

A.D. 64 The Great Fire destroys two-thirds of the city of Rome. Universally loathed emperor Nero is blamed for doing nothing to stop it.

A.D. 64 OR 65 St. Peter is crucified, upside down, at the Circus of Nero, on the future site of Vatican City.

A.D. 72–80 To satisfy the public's growing appetite for blood sport, the Colosseum is built.

A.D. 98–117 The reign of Trajan. The empire reaches its zenith; the power of Rome extends throughout Europe and on every shore of the Mediterranean.

3RD CENTURY A.D. During the "troubled century," Rome loses territory to barbarian invaders.

313 Constantine legalizes Christianity.

330 Byzantium (modern Istanbul) is renamed Constantinople and becomes the new capital of the Roman Empire.

5TH CENTURY A power vacuum leaves Rome defenseless. The city takes a beating from repeated barbarian invasions. Historians cite A.D. 476 as the end of the Western Empire.

7TH–9TH CENTURIES The popes govern a small and scattered population in Rome. The structures of antiquity begin to fall into ruin.

9TH–11TH CENTURIES A conflict-ridden "alliance" between the popes and the Holy Roman

Empire brings centuries of bloody warfare.

11TH–13TH CENTURIES The popes—now essentially princes, descended from Italian nobility—use their influence to extend the reign of the Church throughout Italy.

1303–1377 Temporary removal of the papacy from Rome to Avignon.

1508 Michelangelo begins his frescoes in the Sistine Chapel.

1527 Charles V sacks Rome; the city is held hostage for 7 months.

1555 Roman Jews are ordered to live in the Ghetto.

1590S–1650S The baroque period flourishes: Caravaggio, Borromini, and Bernini lavish their talents on churches, piazzas, and fountains.

1798 Pope ousted by the invading French army.

1848 Rebels declare "the Roman Republic," which is quashed by French troops.

1870 Rome becomes the capital of a newly united Italy.

1922 Mussolini makes the "March on Rome" by train.

1929 Vatican City becomes a sovereign state with the signing of the Lateran Treaty.

1944 Rome is liberated from the Nazis.

1946 The *Repubblica Italiana* is created, ending the reign of the Savoia monarchs.

2001 The richest man in Italy, media tycoon Silvio Berlusconi, is elected prime minister for the second time. (He was prime minister very briefly in the 1990s.) He was replaced by Romano Prodi in 2006.

2001 AS Roma wins the *scudetto*, Italy's prized football (soccer) championship, for the third time.

2005 Pope John Paul II dies at the age of 84 after serving for 27 years. He is replaced by Pope Benedict XVI.

2006 Italia defeats France to win the World Cup. Rome is the epicenter of nationwide revelry.

2008 Berlusconi is voted back in as prime minister, for a third time.

Roman Architecture

The architecture of Rome ranges from Roman temples and Byzantine basilicas to Renaissance churches, baroque palaces, and Fascist-era behemoths. Here is a brief overview.

Ancient Rome (6th c. B.C.– 5th c. A.D.)
Everyone knows that arches and columns were the backbones of Roman buildings, but what about the rest of the buildings' structures?

Some guidelines for making sense of the ruins:

- The lower the base of a building, the older its date; street level in Rome has risen about 9m (30 ft.)

since ancient times. (Roman temples, such as the Pantheon, are a confusing exception to this rule, as temples were built on high podiums that are now flush with modern street level.)

- Round or irregular holes in ancient ruins indicate where metal has been removed (such as lead clamps that held a building together, or iron hooks that held decorations like sculpture or marble revetment).

- Rectangular holes are called "put-log holes," where beams were placed for scaffolding or to support a higher floor.

- Republican architecture was more modest than Imperial. Ruins with simple rectangular plans and plain tufa construction normally predate ruins with heavy marble or intricate vaulting.

- The use of concrete was perfected in the 1st century B.C.; any building utilizing concrete dates after that century.

- As lovely as they look to us today, brick walls never went naked in ancient Rome; they were always covered with marble paneling or stucco.

Early Christian & Romanesque (5th–9th c. A.D.)
The focus is on the interior. Churches are like geodes, with plain brick facades and dazzling jewel-tone mosaics inside.

Medieval (9th–14th c.)
The Middle Ages have largely disappeared from the architectural record

in Rome. Santa Maria Sopra Minerva is the city's only Gothic church, its pointed arches and soaring vaults emphasizing heaven.

Renaissance (15th–16th c.)
Characterized by stateliness, symmetry, and a rebirth of the classical orders, the best Roman architecture of this period is at Piazza del Campidoglio and Palazzo Farnese. Painting and sculpture are balanced, harmonious, and idealistic.

Baroque (17th–18th c.)
Think of the baroque as style with a serious caffeine habit—histrionic and playful, it defines the modern look of Rome. Architects like Bernini and Borromini employed such dynamic flourishes as jagged cornices and curvilinear tension (Sant'Agnese in Agone) to enliven monuments and public squares; sculptors (like Bernini) and painters (like Caravaggio) infused their subjects with naturalism and palpable, high-keyed emotion.

Rococo (18th c.)
Florid to the point of being frenzied—the baroque on methamphetamines.

Neoclassical (19th c.)
Safe and sedate, a return to the purest Greek and Roman forms.

Fascist/Rationalist (1920s–40s)
Buildings are bombastic, blocky caricatures of Roman Imperial monuments. Unweathered and insufficiently relieved by negative volume, they come off much harsher than their ancestors.

Useful Phrases

Useful Phrases

ENGLISH	ITALIAN	PRONUNCIATION
Hello/Good morning	**Buongiorno**	bwohn-*djor*-noh
Hello/Good evening	**Buona sera**	bwohn-ah *say*-rah
Good night	**Buona notte**	bwohn-ah *noht*-tay
Goodbye	**Arrivederci (formal)**	ahr-ree-vah-*dehr*-chee
Hi/Bye	**Ciao (or "salve"; informal)**	chow
Yes	**Sì**	see
No	**No**	noh
Please	**Per favore**	pehr fah-*vohr*-eh
Thank you	**Grazie**	*graht*-tzee-yey
You're welcome/ Go ahead	**Prego**	*prey*-go
Do you speak English?	**Parla inglese?**	*pahr*-lah *een*-gleh-zeh?
I don't speak Italian	**Non parlo italiano**	nohn *parl*-loh ee-tah-lyah-**noh**
Excuse me (apologizing, interrupting)	**Mi scusi**	mee skoo-**ze**
Excuse me (getting through a crowd	**Permesso**	pehr-*mehs*-soh
OK (agreeing)	**Va bene**	vah *beh*-neh
Where is . . . ?	**Dov'è . . . ?**	doh-*vey*
the bathroom	il bagno	eel *bahn*-nyoh
a restaurant	un ristorante	oon reest-ohr-*ahnt*-eh
the hospital	l'ospedale	oh-speh-*dah*-leh
a hotel	un albergo	oon ahl-*behr*-goh
How much does it cost?	**Quanto costa?**	*kwan*-toh *coh*-sta
What time is it?	**Che ore sono?**	kay *or*-ay *soh*-noh
The check, please	**Il conto, per favore**	eel *kon*-toh pehr fah-*vohr*-eh
When?	**Quando?**	*kwan*-doh
Yesterday	**Ieri**	ee-*yehr*-ree
Today	**Oggi**	oh-*jee*
Tomorrow	**Domani**	*doh*-mah-nee
Breakfast	**Prima colazione**	*pree*-mah coh-laht-tzee-*ohn*-ay
Lunch	**Pranzo**	*prahn*-zoh
Dinner	**Cena**	*chay*-nah
Monday	**Lunedì**	loo-nay-*dee*
Tuesday	**Martedì**	mart-ay-*dee*
Wednesday	**Mercoledì**	mehr-cohl-ay-*dee*
Thursday	**Giovedì**	joh-vay-*dee*
Friday	**Venerdì**	ven-nehr-*dee*
Saturday	**Sabato**	sah-*bah*-toh

Numbers

1	uno	oo-**noh**
2	due	doo-**ay**
3	tre	**tray**
4	quattro	kwah-**troh**
5	cinque	cheen-**kway**
6	sei	**say**
7	sette	set-**tay**
8	otto	oh-**toh**
9	nove	noh-**vay**
10	dieci	**dee**-ay-chee
11	undici	oon-**dee**-chee
20	venti	**vehn**-tee
21	ventuno	vehn-**toon**-oh
22	venti due	vehn-**tee** doo-ay
30	trenta	**trehn**-tah
40	quaranta	kwah-**rahn**-tah
50	cinquanta	cheen-**kwan**-tah
60	sessanta	sehs-**sahn**-tah
70	settanta	seht-**tahn**-tah
80	ottanta	oht-**tahn**-tah
90	novanta	noh-**vahnt**-tah
100	cento	chen-**toh**
1,000	mille	mee-**lay**
5,000	cinquemila	cheen-**kway** mee-**lah**
10,000	dieci milla	**dee**-ay-chee mee-**lah**

Toll-Free Numbers & Websites

Airlines

AER LINGUS
☎ 800/474-7424 in the U.S.
☎ 01/886-8844 in Ireland
www.aerlingus.com

AIR CANADA
☎ 888/247-2262
www.aircanada.ca

AIR FRANCE
☎ 800/237-2747 in the U.S.
☎ 0820-820-820 in France
www.airfrance.com

AIR MALTA
☎ 800/756-2582 in the U.S.
☎ 356/2169-0890 in Malta
www.airmalta.com

AIR NEW ZEALAND
☎ 800/262-1234 or -2468 in the U.S.
☎ 800/663-5494 in Canada
☎ 0800/737-000 in New Zealand
www.airnewzealand.com

ALITALIA
☎ 800/223-5730 in the U.S.
☎ 8488-65641 in Italy
www.alitalia.it

AMERICAN AIRLINES
☎ 800/433-7300
www.aa.com

AUSTRIAN AIRLINES
☎ 800/843-0002 in the U.S.
☎ 43/(0)5-1789 in Austria
www.aua.com

BMI
No U.S. number
☎ 0870/6070-222 in Britain
www.flybmi.com

BRITISH AIRWAYS
☎ 800/247-9297

☎ 0870/850-9-850 in Britain
www.british-airways.com

CONTINENTAL AIRLINES
☎ 800/525-0280
www.continental.com

DELTA AIR LINES
☎ 800/221-1212
www.delta.com

EASYJET
No U.S. number
www.easyjet.com

IBERIA
☎ 800/772-4642 in the U.S.
☎ 902/400-500 in Spain
www.iberia.com

ICELANDAIR
☎ 800/223-5500 in the U.S.
☎ 354/50-50-100 in Iceland
www.icelandair.is

KLM
☎ 800/374-7747 in the U.S.
☎ 020/4-747-747 in the Netherlands
www.klm.nl

LUFTHANSA
☎ 800/645-3880 in the U.S.
☎ 49/(0)-180-5-838426 in Germany
www.lufthansa.com

NORTHWEST AIRLINES
☎ 800/225-2525
www.nwa.com

OLYMPIC AIRWAYS
☎ 800/223-1226 in the U.S.
☎ 80/111-444-444 in Greece
www.olympic-airways.gr

QANTAS
☎ 800/227-4500 in the U.S.
☎ 612/131313 in Australia
www.qantas.com

SCANDINAVIAN AIRLINES
☎ 800/221-2350 in the U.S.
☎ 0070/727-727 in Sweden
☎ 70/10-20-00 in Denmark
☎ 358/(0)20-386-000 in Finland
☎ 815/200-400 in Norway
www.flysas.com

SINGAPORE AIRLINES
☎ 800/742-3333 in the U.S.
☎ 65/6223-8888 in Singapore
www.singaporeair.com

SWISS INTERNATIONAL AIRLINES
☎ 877/359-7947 in the U.S.
☎ 0848/85-2000 in Switzerland
www.swiss.com

TAP AIR PORTUGAL
☎ 800/221-7370 in the U.S.
☎ 351/21-841-66-00 in Portugal
www.tap-airportugal.com

TURKISH AIRLINES
☎ 800/874-8875 in the U.S.;
212/339-9650 in NY, NJ, CT
☎ 90-212-663-63-00 in Turkey
www.flyturkish.com

UNITED AIRLINES
☎ 800/241-6522
www.united.com

US AIRWAYS
☎ 800/428-4322
www.usairways.com

VIRGIN ATLANTIC AIRWAYS
☎ 800/862-8621 in continental U.S.
☎ 0870/380-2007 in Britain
www.virgin-atlantic.com

Car-Rental Agencies

ADVANTAGE
☎ 800/777-5500
www.arac.com

ALAMO
☎ 800/327-9633
www.alamo.com

AUTO EUROPE
☎ 800/223-5555
www.autoeurope.com

AVIS
☎ 800/331-1212 in continental U.S.
☎ 800/TRY-AVIS in Canada
www.avis.com

BUDGET
☎ 800/527-0700
www.budget.com

DOLLAR
☎ 800/800-4000
www.dollar.com

HERTZ
☎ 800/654-3131
www.hertz.com

KEMWEL HOLIDAY AUTO (KHA)
☎ 800/678-0678
www.kemwel.com

NATIONAL
☎ 800/227-7368
www.nationalcar.com

THRIFTY
☎ 800/367-2277
www.thrifty.com

Index

See also Accommodations and Restaurant indexes, below.

Photo **Credits**

p i, left: © Guy Vandereist/Getty Images; p i, center: © Michelle Garrett/Corbis; p i, right: © Grant Faint/Getty Images; p ii, top: © Hollenbeck Productions; p ii, 2nd from top: © Hollenbeck Productions; p ii, center: © IML Image Group Ltd/Alamy; p ii, 2nd from bottom: © Dallas & John Heaton/SCPhotos/Alamy; p ii, bottom: © Hollenbeck Productions; p iii, top: © PCL/Alamy; p iii, 2nd from top: © Hotel Hassler; p iii, center: © Bettmann/Corbis; p iii, 2nd from bottom: © Hotel de Russie; p iii, bottom: © Araldo de Luca/Corbis; p viii & 1: © John Lawrence/Getty Images; p 4: © Hollenbeck Productions; p 5: © S. Bavister/Robert Harding Picture Library Ltd/Alamy; p 6, top: © Martin Moos/Lonely Planet Images; p 6, bottom: © Hollenbeck Productions; p 7: © Hollenbeck Productions; p 10: © Hollenbeck Productions; p 11: © Image Source/Alamy; p 12: © Sylvain Grandadam/AGE Fotostock; p 13, top: © Hollenbeck Productions; p 13, bottom: © Hollenbeck Productions; p 15: © Oscar Fdez. Santana/AGE Fotostock; p 16: © Alvaro Leiva/AGE Fotostock; p 17: © Hotel Hassler; p 19: © Charles & Josette Lenars/CORBIS; p 20, top: © Francesco Venturi/Corbis; p 20, bottom: © Hollenbeck Productions; p 21: © Hollenbeck Productions; p 23: © Factoria Singular/AGE Fotostock; p 24: © Bettmann/Corbis; p 26, top: © Peter M. Wilson/Alamy; p 26, bottom: © Charles & Josette Lenars/Corbis; p 27: © Hollenbeck Productions; p 30: © A.H.C./AGE Fotostock; p 31: © Doug Scott/AGE Fotostock/SuperStock; p 33, center: © Hollenbeck Productions; p 33, bottom: © David Tomlinson/Lonely Planet Images; p 34: © Hollenbeck Productions; p 35, top: © Massimo Listri/Corbis; p 35, bottom: © DK Images/PhotoLibrary; p 38: © Hollenbeck Productions; p 39, top: © Martin Moos/Lonely Planet Images; p 39, bottom: © Adam Eastland/Alamy; p 42: © Martin Moos/Lonely Planet Images; p 43: © Hollenbeck Productions; p 45: © Hollenbeck Productions; p 47: © Photolibrary; p 49: © IMAGINA The Image Maker/Alamy; p 50: © Hollenbeck Productions; p 51: © IML Image Group Ltd/Alamy; p 53: © Richard T. Nowitz/Corbis; p 54, top: © Hollenbeck Productions; p 54, bottom: © Walker/PhotoLibrary; p 55: © Ian M. Butterfield/Alamy; p 57: © Ted Spiegel/Corbis; p 59: © CuboImages srl/Alamy; p 61: © Gari Wyn Williams/Alamy; p 62: © Max Rossi/Reuters/Corbis; p 63, bottom: © George Atsametakis/IML Image Group/drr.net; p 63, top: © Ted Spiegel/Corbis; p 65, top: © GiovanniDeAngelis/CuboImages; p 65, bottom: © Nordicphotos/Alamy; p 67, bottom: © Hubert Stadler/Corbis; p 68: © Nicolas Sapieha/Corbis; p 69: © Franz-Marc Frei/Corbis; p 71: © Giovanni De Angelis/CuboImages; p 73: © Bill Ross/Corbis; p 74: © Clive Sawyer/Alamy; p 75: © Dallas & John Heaton/SCPhotos/Alamy; p 76: © Martin Moos/Lonely Planet Images; p 81: © Hollenbeck Productions; p 82, top: © Kathy de Witt/Alamy; p 82, bottom: © GiovanniDeAngelis/CuboImages; p 84: © Hollenbeck Productions; p 86: © Owen Franken/Corbis; p 87: © Hollenbeck Productions; p 88: © Al Sogno; p 89: © Hollenbeck Productions; p 92: © Eddie Gerald/Alamy; p 93, top: © John Heseltine/Corbis; p 93, bottom: © Atlantide Phototravel/Corbis; p 95: © Araldo de Luca/Corbis; p 96: © Ruggero Vanni/Corbis; p 97: © Hollenbeck Productions; p 100, top: © Francesco Venturi/Corbis; p 100, bottom: © Hollenbeck Productions; p 101: © PCL/Alamy; p 108: © Checchino Restaurant; p 109: © Hollenbeck Productions;

p 110: © Hollenbeck Productions; p 111: © Digital Vision Ltd./AGE Fotostock; p 113: © Lisa Romerein/Getty Images; p 114: © Hollenbeck Productions; p 115: © Hotel Hassler; p 116: Courtesy of Freni e Frizioni, Roma; p 121: © David Noton/Getty Images; p 122: © Richard T. Nowitz/Corbis; p 123: © Martin Moos/Lonely Planet Images; p 124: © Martin Moos/Lonely Planet Images; p 125: © Bettmann/Corbis; p 126: © Francesco Venturi/Corbis; p 129, top: © Hollenbeck Productions; p 129, bottom: © Hollenbeck Productions; p 130: © John & Lisa Merrill/Corbis; p 131: © Franz-Marc Frei/Corbis; p 132: © Maurizio Brambatti/epa/Corbis; p 133: © Hotel de Russie; p 134: © Aldrovandi Palace Hotel; p 140: Courtesy of Casa Howard, Roma; p 141: Courtesy of Hotel Forte, Roma; p 143: Courtesy of Lord Byron, Roma; p 144, top: Courtesy of Hotel Modigliani, Roma; p 144, bottom: © Martin Moos/Lonely Planet Images; p 145: Courtesy of Portrait Suites, Roma; p 146: Courtesy of Hotel Villa Laetitia, Roma; p 147: © Araldo de Luca/Corbis; p 149: © Roger Wood/Corbis; p 151: © Vanni Archive/Corbis; p 153: © Roger Ressmeyer/Corbis; p 155: © AA World Travel Library/ Alamy; p 157: © Frank Chmura/Alamy; p 158: © Archivo Iconografico, S.A./Corbis; p 159: © David Hanover/Corbis

The new way to
get AROUND town.

Make the most of your stay. Go Day by Day

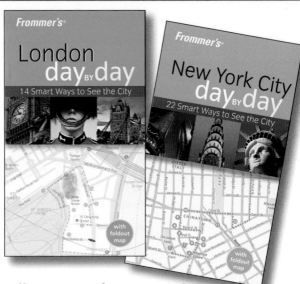

The all-new Day by Day series shows you the best places to visit and the best way to see them.

- Full-color throughout, with hundreds of photos and maps
- Packed with 1–to–3–day itineraries, neighborhood walks, and thematic tours
- Museums, literary haunts, offbeat places, and more
- Star-rated hotel and restaurant listings
- Sturdy foldout map in reclosable plastic wallet
- Foldout front covers with at-a-glance maps and info

The best trips start here. **Frommer's**

Wiley and the Wiley logo are registered trademarks of John Wiley & Sons, Inc. Frommer's is a registered trademark of Arthur Frommer.

A Branded Imprint of ⓦWILEY
Now you know.